REFLECT ⁴

READING & WRITING

CHRISTIEN LEE

**NATIONAL
GEOGRAPHIC
LEARNING**

Australia · Brazil · Mexico · Singapore · United Kingdom · United States

National Geographic Learning,
a Cengage Company

Reflect 4 Reading & Writing
Author: Christien Lee

Publisher: Sherrise Roehr
Executive Editor: Laura Le Dréan
Managing Editor: Angel Alonso
Director of Global Marketing: Ian Martin
Product Marketing Manager: Tracy Baillie
Senior Content Project Manager: Mark Rzeszutek
Media Researcher: Jeff Millies
Art Director: Brenda Carmichael
Senior Designer: Lisa Trager
Operations Coordinator: Hayley Chwazik-Gee
Manufacturing Buyer: Mary Beth Hennebury
Composition: MPS Limited

For permission to use material from this text or product,
submit all requests online at **cengage.com/permissions**
Further permissions questions can be emailed to
permissionrequest@cengage.com

Student Book ISBN: 978-0-357-44851-9
Student Book with Online Practice: 978-0-357-44857-1

National Geographic Learning
200 Pier 4 Boulevard
Boston, MA 02210

Locate your local office at **international.ceng**

Visit National Geographic Learning online a
Visit our corporate website at **www.cenga**

D1089133

Printed in Mexico
Print Number: 01   Print Year: 2021

SCOPE AND SEQUENCE

<table>
<tr><td colspan="2"></td><td>READING & VOCABULARY EXPANSION</td></tr>
</table>

WORLDS WITHIN WORLDS
SOCIOLOGY
page 2

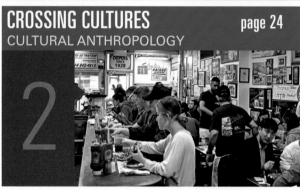

Video: Amber Case: Caring for Your Second Self

Reading 1: Real and Virtual Communities

Reading 2: The Power of Two

Recognize how information is supported

Using a dictionary: Antonyms

CROSSING CULTURES
CULTURAL ANTHROPOLOGY
page 24

Video: What Is "Culture?"

Reading 1: Cultural Confusion?

Reading 2: What's in a Name?

Understand unfamiliar vocabulary

Base words and affixes

PLAYING WITH DESIGN
DESIGN
page 46

Video: Rethinking Waste

Reading 1: Serious Problems, Playful Solutions

Reading 2: The Power of a Nudge

Make inferences

Greek and Latin roots: *mot* and *cycl*

OUR ROBOT FUTURE
SCIENCE
page 68

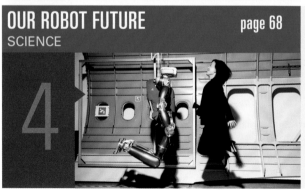

Video: Rise of the Robobees

Reading 1: Robots: From Fiction to Fact

Reading 2: A Robot Future? Not So Fast!; AI for a Better Tomorrow

Take notes

Collocations: Adjective + preposition

WRITING	GRAMMAR	CRITICAL THINKING	REFLECT ACTIVITIES
Organize an opinion essay	Adjective clauses	Understand a writer's purpose	▶ Rank reasons for joining online communities ▶ Consider the value of being part of a community ▶ Evaluate the benefits of multicultural cities ▶ Compare the benefits of different communities ▶ **UNIT TASK** Write an opinion essay about online communities
Add supporting ideas and details	The passive voice	Evaluate the strength of an argument	▶ Relate to different aspects of culture ▶ Evaluate opinions about culture ▶ Consider how culture can influence a brand ▶ Synthesize ideas about culture ▶ **UNIT TASK** Write a descriptive essay about cultural symbols
Describe a process	Noun phrases	Connect new ideas to what you know	▶ Consider the importance of play ▶ Relate ideas about play to your life ▶ Consider how design can change behavior ▶ Create a design to change behavior ▶ **UNIT TASK** Write a description of a diagram
Write a summary	Noun clauses	Support your opinions	▶ Consider what robots can do ▶ Discuss fictional robots ▶ Predict the abilities of future robots ▶ Support your opinion about AI ▶ **UNIT TASK** Write a summary

5 THERE IS NO PLANET B
TECHNOLOGY & THE ENVIRONMENT

page 90

Video: What Is Renewable Energy?

Reading 1: Cool Invention?

Reading 2: Innovative Ideas for the Environment

Understand references within a text

Using a dictionary: Synonyms

6 SAVVY SHOPPERS
BUSINESS

page 112

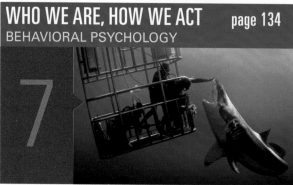

Video: Vote with Your Wallet

Reading 1: Keeping Customers Happy

Reading 2: Be a Better Buyer

Recognize coherence and cohesion

Compound words

7 WHO WE ARE, HOW WE ACT
BEHAVIORAL PSYCHOLOGY

page 134

Video: Cakes of Deception

Reading 1: Personality: What Type Are You?

Reading 2: The Psychology of Giving

Recognize cause and effect

Word forms: Using the suffixes *-or*, *-er,* and *-ion*

8 LEARN TO CHANGE
EDUCATION

page 156

Video: More than Peach

Reading 1: Young Changemakers

Reading 2: A Step to College Success

Analyze visual information

Polysemy (Multiple-meaning words)

Vocabulary Expansion Activities   page 178

Appendices   page 186

Index of Exam Skills and Tasks   page 191

Credits   page 192

WRITING	GRAMMAR	CRITICAL THINKING	REFLECT ACTIVITIES
Organize a problem-solution essay	Pronouns and related words	Evaluate solutions	▶ Consider the impact of inventions ▶ Discuss the pros and cons of "green" actions ▶ Consider what makes a solution innovative ▶ Evaluate innovations ▶ **UNIT TASK** Write a problem-solution essay about an environmental issue
Organize a review	Comparatives, *as . . . as,* superlatives	Understand the order of events	▶ Consider what customers want ▶ Evaluate your shopping experiences ▶ Compare shopping habits ▶ Synthesize ideas about buyers and sellers ▶ **UNIT TASK** Write a review of a product or service
Organize a compare-contrast essay	Compare-and-contrast connectors	Connect information to personal experiences	▶ Compare and contrast personality types ▶ Consider your behavior in different situations ▶ Evaluate reasons why people help others ▶ Consider the effects of cognitive biases ▶ **UNIT TASK** Write a compare-contrast essay about experiences
Describe data in charts	Non-defining adjective clauses	Notice similarities and differences	▶ Assess the qualities of changemakers ▶ Describe the impact of a changemaker ▶ Consider the effects of life changes ▶ Apply advice to different situations ▶ **UNIT TASK** Write a description of visuals

CONNECT TO IDEAS

Reflect Reading & Writing features relevant, global content to engage students while helping them acquire the academic language and skills they need. Specially-designed activities give students the opportunity to reflect on and connect ideas and language to their academic, work, and personal lives.

Academic, real-world passages invite students to explore the world while building reading skills and providing ideas for writing.

Each unit starts with a **high-interest video** to introduce the theme and generate pre-reading discussion.

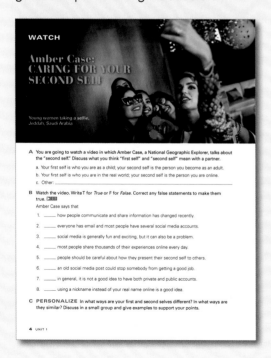

CONNECT TO ACADEMIC SKILLS

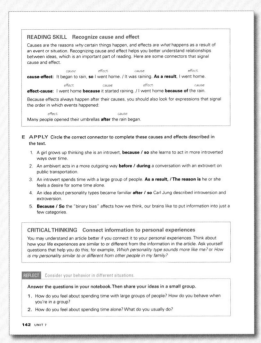

Focused **reading skills** help create confident academic readers.

Reflect activities give students opportunities to think critically about what they are learning and check their understanding.

Clear writing models and **analyze the model** activities give students a strong framework to improve their writing.

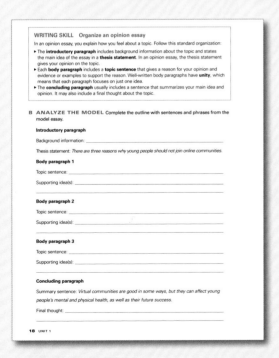

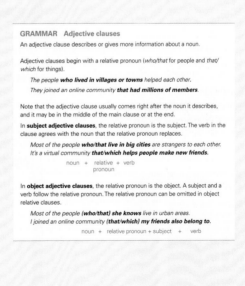

A **step-by-step approach** to the **writing process** along with relevant grammar helps students complete the final writing task with confidence.

CONNECT TO ACHIEVEMENT

Reflect at the end of the unit is an opportunity for formative assessment. Students review the skills and vocabulary they have gained.

DIGITAL RESOURCES

TEACH lively, engaging lessons that get students to participate actively. The Classroom Presentation Tool helps teachers to present the Student's Book pages, play audio and video, and increase participation by providing a central focus for the class.

LEARN AND TRACK with Online Practice and Student's eBook. For students, the mobile-friendly platform reinforces learning through additional practice. For instructors, progress-tracking is made easy through the shared gradebook.

ASSESS learner performance and progress with the ExamView® Assessment Suite. For assessment, teachers create and customize tests and quizzes easily using the ExamView® Assessment Suite, available online.

ACKNOWLEDGMENTS

The Authors and Publisher would like to acknowledge the teachers around the world who participated in the development of *Reflect*.

A special thanks to our Advisory Board for their valuable input during the development of this series.

ADVISORY BOARD

Dr. Mansoor S. Almalki, Taif University, Saudi Arabia; **John Duplice**, Sophia University, Japan; **Heba Elhadary**, Gulf University for Science and Technology, Kuwait; **Hind Elyas**, Niagara College, Saudi Arabia; **Cheryl House**, ILSC Education Group, Canada; **Xiao Luo**, BFUS International, China; **Daniel L. Paller,** Kinjo Gakuin University, Japan; **Ray Purdy**, ELS Education Services, USA; **Sarah Symes,** Cambridge Street Upper School, USA.

GLOBAL REVIEWERS

ASIA

Michael Crawford, Dokkyo University, Japan; **Ronnie Hill**, RMIT University Vietnam, Vietnam; **Aaron Nurse**, Golden Path Academics, Vietnam; **Simon Park**, Zushi Kaisei, Japan; **Aunchana Punnarungsee**, Majeo University, Thailand.

LATIN AMERICA AND THE CARIBBEAN

Leandro Aguiar, inFlux, Brazil; **Sonia Albertazzi-Osorio**, Costa Rica Institute of Technology, Costa Rica; **Auricea Bacelar**, Top Seven Idiomas, Brazil; **Natalia Benavides**, Universidad de Los Andes, Colombia; **James Bonilla**, Global Language Training UK, Colombia; **Diego Bruekers Deschamp**, Inglês Express, Brazil; **Josiane da Rosa**, Hello Idiomas, Brazil; **Marcos de Campos Bueno**, It's Cool International, Brazil; **Sophia De Carvalho**, Ingles Express, Brazil; **André Luiz dos Santos**, IFG, Brazil; **Oscar Gomez-Delgado**, Universidad de los Andes, Colombia; **Ruth Elizabeth Hibas**, Inglês Express, Brazil; **Rebecca Ashley Hibas**, Inglês Express, Brazil; **Cecibel Juliao**, UDELAS University, Panama; **Rosa Awilda López Fernández**, School of Languages UNAPEC University, Dominican Republic; **Isabella Magalhães**, Fluent English Pouso Alegre, Brazil; **Gabrielle Marchetti**, Teacher's House, Brazil; **Sabine Mary**, INTEC, Dominican Republic; **Miryam Morron**, Corporación Universitaria Americana, Colombia; **Mary Ruth Popov**, Ingles Express, Ltda., Brazil; **Leticia Rodrigues Resende**, Brazil; **Margaret Simons**, English Center, Brazil.

MIDDLE EAST

Abubaker Alhitty, University of Bahrain, Bahrain; **Jawaria Iqbal**, Saudi Arabia; **Rana Khan**, Algonquin College, Kuwait; **Mick King**, Community College of Qatar, Qatar; **Seema Jaisimha Terry**, German University of Technology, Oman.

USA AND CANADA

Thomas Becskehazy, Arizona State University, AZ; **Robert Bushong**, University of Delaware, DE; **Ashley Fifer**, Nassau Community College, NY; **Sarah Arva Grosik**, University of Pennsylvania, PA; **Carolyn Ho**, Lone Star College-CyFair, TX; **Zachary Johnsrud**, Norquest College, Canada; **Caitlin King**, IUPUI, IN; **Andrea Murau Haraway**, Global Launch / Arizona State University, AZ; **Bobbi Plante**, Manitoba Institute of Trades and Technology, Canada; **Michael Schwartz**, St. Cloud State University, MN; **Pamela Smart-Smith**, Virginia Tech, VA; **Kelly Smith**, English Language Institute, UCSD Extension, CA; **Karen Vallejo**, University of California, CA.

WORLDS WITHIN WORLDS

A *paifang*, or traditional Chinese gateway, London, UK

IN THIS UNIT

▶ Rank reasons for joining online communities

▶ Consider the value of being part of a community

▶ Evaluate the benefits of multicultural cities

▶ Compare the benefits of different communities

▶ Write an opinion essay about online communities

SKILLS

READING
Recognize how information is supported

WRITING
Organize an opinion essay

GRAMMAR
Adjective clauses

CRITICAL THINKING
Understand a writer's purpose

CONNECT TO THE TOPIC

1. Do you think you would enjoy living in or near a place like the one in the photo?

2. In your opinion, which is more important: the people you live near or the place you live in?

3

WATCH

Amber Case: CARING FOR YOUR SECOND SELF

Young women taking a selfie,
Jeddah, Saudi Arabia

A You are going to watch a video in which Amber Case, a National Geographic Explorer, talks about the "second self." Discuss what you think "first self" and "second self" mean with a partner.

a. Your first self is who you are as a child; your second self is the person you become as an adult.

b. Your first self is who you are in the real world; your second self is the person you are online.

c. Other: _____

B Watch the video. Write T for *True* or F for *False*. Correct any false statements to make them true. ▶ 1.1

Amber Case says that

1. _____ how people communicate and share information has changed recently.

2. _____ everyone has email and most people have several social media accounts.

3. _____ social media is generally fun and exciting, but it can also be a problem.

4. _____ most people share thousands of their experiences online every day.

5. _____ people should be careful about how they present their second self to others.

6. _____ an old social media post could stop somebody from getting a good job.

7. _____ in general, it is not a good idea to have both private and public accounts.

8. _____ using a nickname instead of your real name online is a good idea.

C PERSONALIZE In what ways are your first and second selves different? In what ways are they similar? Discuss in a small group and give examples to support your points.

PREPARE TO READ

A VOCABULARY Read the sentences. Then write the words in bold next to their definitions.

▸ More and more young people are using social media, but some adults worry about this **trend**. They believe that children will lose their right to **privacy**. Do you think this is a problem?

▸ What is your perfect **community**: a busy **urban** area with many people around, somewhere quiet and **rural** that is **surrounded** by nature, or somewhere else?

▸ Do you believe computers may soon become so **advanced** that online **virtual** communities will become more fun and enjoyable than real ones?

▸ Do you agree that technology is becoming faster and more **powerful**? Does this create a **paradox** by making our lives busier but not easier?

1. _____ (n) a situation that is continuing to change or develop

2. _____ (n) a place where people live; a group of people with similar interests

3. _____ (adj) having something all around it

4. _____ (adj) relating to the countryside

5. _____ (adj) relating to towns or cities

6. _____ (adj) done or seen on the Internet or a computer

7. _____ (adj) very strong and effective; able to do a lot

8. _____ (adj) very modern; recently developed or improved

9. _____ (n) a situation that is hard to understand because it has two opposite qualities

10. _____ (n) freedom to keep personal information secret

B PERSONALIZE Discuss the questions in activity A in a small group. Explain your answers.

REFLECT Rank reasons for joining online communities.

You are going to read about real and virtual communities. Look at the list of reasons why people join virtual communities. Then discuss other reasons with a partner and add them to the list. Put the reasons in order from most common (1) to least common (6).

_____ to chat with family   _____ to look for a job   _____
_____ to learn something   _____ to make friends   _____

READ

Telegraph station,
Nantucket Island,
Massachusetts,
USA, 1908

A PREDICT Look at the title and
photos. Then skim the article and
tell a partner what topic or topics
you think the article will discuss.
Check your predictions after
you read.

B MAIN IDEAS Read the article.
Then check the four main ideas.

1. _____ It can be hard to connect
with other people if you
live in a large city.

2. _____ Virtual communities have
a long history beginning
in the late 1800s.

3. _____ Citizen's Band was
an earlier form of
communication than
cell phones.

4. _____ Virtual communities have
some advantages over
real-life communities.

5. _____ People who join many
online communities
usually have
many friends.

6. _____ In the future, virtual
communities are likely to
become more important.

REAL AND VIRTUAL COMMUNITIES

1   For most of history, people lived in **rural** areas in small groups of up to 150 people. Then about 9,500 years ago, villages and small towns began to develop. **Communities** such as these were generally safer, and people were able to help one another by sharing food and other useful items. As time passed, **urban** living provided other advantages, including better jobs, schools, and health care. Larger towns also gave people more chances to meet and be with others. This is important because, as Aristotle[1] and other great thinkers have said, the nature[2] of humans is to be social.

2   Today, according to the United Nations, over half of the world's population currently lives in towns, cities, and megacities[3] such as Shanghai, Mexico City, or Istanbul. But this development has created a strange **paradox**. Although social opportunities are one reason people choose to live in large communities, research suggests that city life can be lonely. People may be **surrounded** by millions of others, but they're often strangers to each other.

3   This paradox may explain why **virtual** communities are so popular. On the Internet, people can join online communities and make virtual friends. These online communities have an advantage over real ones since people can join them from all over the world without leaving home. And everyone can easily find groups of people who have similar interests and spend time with them.

---

[1] **Aristotle** a philosopher and writer from ancient Greece

[2] **nature** (n) the basic quality of someone or something

[3] **megacity** (n) a city where more than 10 million people live

THE SURPRISING HISTORY OF VIRTUAL COMMUNITIES

4   One of the earliest virtual communities began in the 1860s, when people sent messages across long distances by telegraph. During their free time, telegraph operators—separated by hundreds or thousands of miles—chatted, joked, and even played games with each other. Most of these operators never met, but over time, friendships developed. Sometimes hundreds of operators all used the telegraph at the same time—creating the very first virtual meetings.

Trucker using a CB radio

Young people using a computer in Miramas, France, 1989

Home page of the role-playing web site, Second Life

5   Before cell phones existed, Citizen's Band (CB) radio was an easy way to communicate over short distances from a car or other vehicle. CB became a popular **trend** in the 1960s in the United States among people who traveled around a lot, such as truck drivers or salespeople. By the 1970s, many CB communities had developed. Members often had CB names, called "handles," and they used special language such as "negatory" for *no* or "copy that" for *I understand*. These expressions are similar to the modern usernames and Internet slang (e.g., "LOL" for "laugh out loud") of online communities.

6   The first popular online communities developed in the 1980s. Computers were not very **powerful** yet, so people could post messages and share news and stories but not music or photos. Still, people loved being able to make friends online and then hang out with them. A very early example of this type of virtual community was The WELL. Even though it's now over 35 years old, this community is still important to its members. In fact, when The WELL was available for sale in 2012, some of them decided to buy it and keep it running.

7   As technology became more powerful, online communities became more **advanced**. In the early 2000s, Second Life became popular because it was so much fun. Users could explore a virtual 3-D world, buy things with virtual money, listen to music, and even play online sports. They could create their own virtual communities within the world, too. This helped Second Life become one of the first online communities that was important for education and business.

8   These days, there are thousands of virtual communities and that number keeps growing. Some have millions or billions of active members. Many people think this will continue and, in the future, virtual communities will become even more important. However, others worry about problems with these communities. In particular, they are concerned that posting personal information online might lead to a loss of **privacy**. So perhaps the future will be more like the past: People will spend most of their time in real communities.

---

⁴**hang out with** (v phr) spend time with

C DETAILS Complete the time line. Each answer is two words.

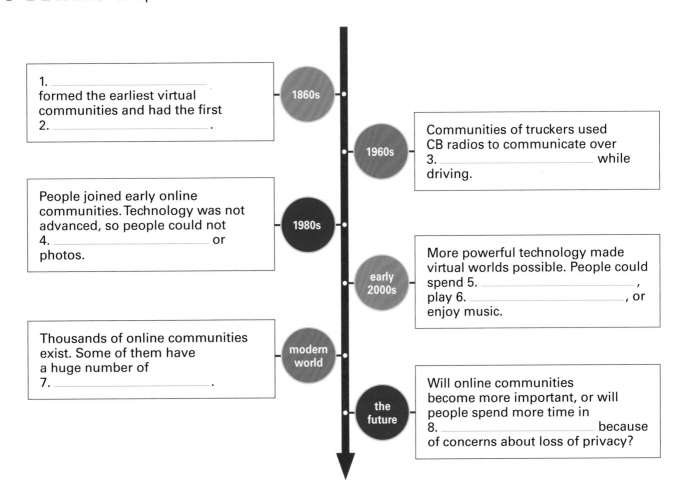

1. _____ formed the earliest virtual communities and had the first 2. _____ .

1860s

1960s Communities of truckers used CB radios to communicate over 3. _____ while driving.

People joined early online communities. Technology was not advanced, so people could not 4. _____ or photos.

1980s

early 2000s More powerful technology made virtual worlds possible. People could spend 5. _____ , play 6. _____ , or enjoy music.

Thousands of online communities exist. Some of them have a huge number of 7. _____ .

modern world

the future Will online communities become more important, or will people spend more time in 8. _____ because of concerns about loss of privacy?

CRITICAL THINKING   Understand a writer's purpose

Good writers have a reason or purpose for choosing information they include in a text. Understanding a writer's purpose can help you understand the overall message better. Writers don't usually directly explain why they include specific information, so you need to think critically in order to understand the purpose.

D DETAILS Choose the reason you think the writer mentions each piece of information.

1. The words of Aristotle

    a. To support the idea that meeting others is one benefit of larger towns

    b. To explain why great thinkers usually live in urban areas, not rural ones

2. Internet slang

    a. To argue that many Internet slang expressions come from CB slang

    b. To suggest that virtual communities often develop slang expressions

3. The sale of The WELL

    a. To explain that virtual communities are very expensive to buy

    b. To show how important this community has been to its members

4. The number of members that some online communities have today

    a. To explain why most virtual communities are successful

    b. To emphasize the popularity of virtual communities

READING SKILL Recognize how information is supported

As you read, it's important to recognize how a writer supports their opinions and ideas. In formal writing, a writer may use:

1. citations or specific references   *According to the World Health Organization, . . .*
2. general research   *A recent study suggests that . . .*
3. statistics   *Over 40 percent of companies . . .*
4. examples   *One early example was. . .*
5. reasons   *This was an important change because . . .*
6. personal anecdotes   *I had this experience once in college . . .*

A writer may choose not to include support for historical information, events, or ideas that everyone knows are true.

E APPLY Review the reading and decide what method the writer uses to support each idea. Choose the correct method from the Reading Skill box (1–5) or write NS for *No Support*.

a. _____ Larger communities are safer than smaller ones. (paragraph 1)

b. _____ Around the world, most people live in cities these days. (paragraph 2)

c. _____ People who live in cities or other urban areas can feel lonely. (paragraph 2)

d. _____ Online communities may be better than real communities. (paragraph 3)

e. _____ Members of virtual communities may use special expressions. (paragraph 5)

REFLECT Consider the value of being part of a community.

Make notes to answer these questions. Then discuss your ideas in a small group.

1. Aristotle, the philosopher mentioned in the article, wrote that the nature of humans is to be social. Do you agree? Explain.

2. Do you think being part of an online community is a good way to meet and spend time with people? Explain.

PREPARE TO READ

A VOCABULARY Read the paragraphs. Write the words in bold next to their definitions.

▶ **Multicultural** cities such as Dubai, São Paulo, Shanghai, and Toronto are well known for their diversity. Many people in these cities are **bilingual** and may speak different languages at work and at home. Because they're used to interacting with people from many cultures, they're often **open to** new ideas and experiences.

▶ Doctors **warn** that life can be difficult for older people because their bodies and brains become less **flexible**. In addition, loneliness can be a problem. Regular physical and **mental** activity and socializing with others can help them **function** more effectively.

▶ Some people argue that going on a "digital fast" can be **beneficial**. They say that not using technology for a period of time **boosts** their mood and makes them feel happier. They also say they **accomplish** a lot because they have more time to work on important things.

1. _____ (adj) comfortable with; willing to try

2. _____ (adj) including people from different countries

3. _____ (adj) able to change easily to fit into new situations

4. _____ (adj) helpful, useful, or positive

5. _____ (adj) able to speak two languages well

6. _____ (adj) related to the mind or thinking

7. _____ (v) to achieve something after doing it for a long time

8. _____ (v) to work or perform in the correct way

9. _____ (v) to improve or increase something

10. _____ (v) to tell somebody about a possible danger or problem

B PERSONALIZE Discuss these questions with a partner.

1. Do you think you are **mentally flexible** and **open to** new experiences? Explain.
2. What are some benefits of being **bilingual** that you know about or can imagine?

REFLECT   Evaluate the benefits of multicultural cities.

Before you read about the benefits of being multicultural and living in a multicultural city, write notes to answer these questions. Then discuss your ideas in a small group.

1. What is the most multicultural city that you know? In what ways is it multicultural?
2. In what ways might visiting or living in that city be beneficial?

THE POWER OF TWO

Students take part in an English as a Second Language program in Philadelphia, Pennsylvania, USA.

A PREDICT Look at the photo. Read the title and paragraph 1. Complete the sentence in your own words and then discuss your ideas with a partner.

The article is probably called *The Power of Two* because it focuses on

_____.

1   These days, most of us have two selves: the person we are in the real world and the person we are in online communities. One thing is true, though, for almost everyone—we want to be better, more successful versions of ourselves. Many of us want to improve our memory, learn to think better, earn more money, make more friends, and be more creative. It may sound almost impossible to achieve these things, but studies suggest there is a surprisingly simple way to **accomplish** all of them: become fluent in two languages.

2   Knowing two languages was not always considered useful. In fact, in some parts of the world, it was considered harmful for children to be **bilingual**. Families with parents from two different cultures were sometimes **warned** not to let their children speak both languages. According to some experts at the time, bilingual children might experience problems. One professor at Cambridge University even argued that the brains of bilingual boys and girls might develop half as much as the brains of monolingual children. Some studies suggested that children who were raised in bilingual families might grow up to be less intelligent or find it hard to control their behavior. More recent studies have suggested that these early theories were not just incorrect but completely backward[1]: Speaking two languages is actually **beneficial**.

3   Studies suggest that being bilingual can **boost** people's ability to **function** effectively by improving "executive function" in the brain. This is the name for a set of **mental** skills that help us remember new things, think in **flexible** ways, and control our behavior. Executive function helps us set goals, make plans, and get things done. People who are bilingual may do well at work and in school because they have good working memory[2], can think about information in different ways, and can stay focused on a task. One study suggests that during their careers, people who know two languages might earn an average of about $125,000 more than those who know just one. And the benefits are not just monetary. Studies show that being bilingual may even protect against the kinds of mental problems that can affect older people.

---

[1]**backward** (adj) not advanced

[2]**working memory** (n) the part of a person's memory that stores information used to deal with the current situation or task

4   For obvious reasons, many people who know two languages fluently also know two cultures well. For example, someone from a Japanese-Italian family who grows up bilingual not only speaks both languages, but probably has a deep understanding of both cultures, as well. And research shows that being bicultural, or being a member of two different cultures, has similar benefits to being bilingual. Those who are bicultural may know more people and have greater opportunities to make friends. They may also be more **open to** other cultures and ideas, and they might find it easier to see things from different points of view. Studies also show that bicultural people are often creative and accomplish a lot in their lives and careers.

5   How does this help people who are neither bilingual nor bicultural? Interestingly, studies suggest that being *fully* bilingual is unnecessary. Just the process of learning a new language is beneficial because it boosts executive function. Visiting or moving to a new country or to a more **multicultural** community within your own country are excellent ways to experience new cultures. In fact, simply trying to be more open to other cultures and ideas seems beneficial. In time, future research may even show that learning about and experiencing new cultures by spending time in virtual communities is equally beneficial.

B MAIN IDEAS Check (✓) the four statements that summarize the main ideas. The other statements either summarize less important points or describe ideas the writer does not mention.

1. _____ Being bilingual is good, but knowing more than two languages is bad.

2. _____ Creative people are open to meeting people who work in different jobs.

3. _____ It's beneficial to be open to others and to have good executive function.

4. _____ Bilingual people earn more money over their careers than other people.

5. _____ Past ideas about being bilingual are very different from current ones.

6. _____ People who aren't bilingual or bicultural can also improve their abilities.

7. _____ It costs a lot of money for somebody to learn to become fully bilingual.

8. _____ Being bilingual or bicultural helps people accomplish things in their lives.

C DETAILS Write the paragraph number where each statement could be added.

___4___ a. For example, one study showed bicultural people did well on creativity tests.

_____ b. So, visiting or moving to another place may not even be necessary.

_____ c. Bilingual people may still experience issues related to aging but may get them later in life.

_____ d. Some members of virtual communities have several online selves.

_____ e. It was felt that being bilingual might lead to serious emotional problems.

_____ f. This is because some employers pay more for those skills because they believe they are valuable.

D APPLY How does the writer support their ideas? Find and underline one example of each method in the reading. Write the paragraph number where the example appears.

a. _____ With a citation

b. _____ With general research

c. _____ With a statistic

d. _____ With an example

e. _____ With a reason

Compare the benefits of different communities.

Complete the chart with your ideas. Then discuss these questions in a small group.

1. Which benefits of the two kinds of communities are the same? Which are different?

2. Which experience do you think is more beneficial overall?

Benefits of being part of a virtual community	Benefits of being part of a bilingual or bicultural community

Bilingual signs in Shinjuku Station, the world's busiest train station, Tokyo, Japan

WRITE

College students passing time between classes

UNIT TASK Write an opinion essay about online communities.

You are going to write an essay in response to the question: "Do you agree or disagree that joining online communities is good for teenagers?" Use the ideas, vocabulary, and skills from the unit.

WRITING TIP

In an opinion essay, you may want to use an anecdote—an example or story from your personal life—to support your ideas. Personal anecdotes can engage the reader and make them feel a connection to your topic.

Be sure that your anecdote always relates clearly to the topic of your essay. Refer back to your anecdote at different points in your essay to maintain your readers' interest.

A MODEL Read the essay. How does the writer support his ideas? Find and underline one example of each method. Write the number of the method next to the sentence.

1. a citation or specific reference
2. general research
3. an example
4. a reason
5. an anecdote or personal story

Online Communities: Not for Young People

In my view, young people often want to join virtual communities because their friends are members. I understand this reason, but I think online communities can affect children and teenagers negatively. There are three reasons why young people should not join online communities.

First, studies show that using social media a lot can cause emotional problems. People that spend a lot of time in online communities are more likely to feel worried and unhappy. Part of the problem is a feeling called FOMO, or "fear of missing out." Many people post stories about exciting things in their lives. When someone else reads these posts, they may feel their own life is not exciting enough. I believe this is especially true for young people.

Second, many young people I know spend a lot of time looking at social media on their phones and tablets. According to a recent documentary about this topic, looking at screens too much can make it harder for people to sleep. The documentary explained that young people, in particular, need plenty of sleep. One expert in the film said that not sleeping enough can cause serious health problems, including stress.

Finally, spending too much time online can have a negative impact on young people's education. My parents always say that my sisters and I enjoy chatting online with our friends more than studying or doing homework. Recent articles make the same point about online communities. They suggest that children who don't study enough often find it hard to be successful in the future.

Virtual communities are good in some ways, but they can affect young people's mental and physical health, as well as their future success. As a result, I feel strongly that parents and other adults should limit how much time children and teenagers spend in these communities.

WRITING SKILL   Organize an opinion essay

In an opinion essay, you explain how you feel about a topic. Follow this standard organization:

▶ The **introductory paragraph** includes background information about the topic and states the main idea of the essay in a **thesis statement**. In an opinion essay, the thesis statement gives your opinion on the topic.

▶ Each **body paragraph** includes a **topic sentence** that gives a reason for your opinion and evidence or examples to support the reason. Well-written body paragraphs have **unity**, which means that each paragraph focuses on just one idea.

▶ The **concluding paragraph** usually includes a sentence that summarizes your main idea and opinion. It may also include a final thought about the topic.

B ANALYZE THE MODEL Complete the outline with sentences and phrases from the model essay.

Introductory paragraph

Background information: _____

Thesis statement: *There are three reasons why young people should not join online communities.*

Body paragraph 1

Topic sentence: _____

Supporting idea(s): _____

_____

Body paragraph 2

Topic sentence: _____

Supporting idea(s): _____

_____

Body paragraph 3

Topic sentence: _____

Supporting idea(s): _____

_____

Concluding paragraph

Summary sentence: *Virtual communities are good in some ways, but they can affect young people's mental and physical health, as well as their future success.*

Final thought: _____

_____

GRAMMAR Adjective clauses

An adjective clause describes or gives more information about a noun.

Adjective clauses begin with a relative pronoun (*who/that* for people and *that/ which* for things).

> The people **who lived in villages or towns** helped each other.
> They joined an online community **that had millions of members**.

Note that the adjective clause usually comes right after the noun it describes, and it may be in the middle of the main clause or at the end.

In **subject adjective clauses**, the relative pronoun is the subject. The verb in the clause agrees with the noun that the relative pronoun replaces.

> *Most of the people **who/that live in big cities** are strangers to each other.*
> *It's a virtual community **that/which helps people make new friends**.*

> noun   +   relative   +   verb
>   pronoun

In **object adjective clauses**, the relative pronoun is the object. A subject and a verb follow the relative pronoun. The relative pronoun can be omitted in object relative clauses.

> *Most of the people **(who/that) she knows** live in urban areas.*
> *I joined an online community **(that/which) my friends also belong to**.*

> noun   +   relative pronoun + subject   +   verb

C   GRAMMAR Find and underline the three adjective clauses in the model essay. Circle the noun that the clause describes.

D   GRAMMAR Underline the adjective clauses. Then check (✓) where each adjective clause appears: in the middle of the main clause or at the end.

1. He joined an online community that has millions of members.   ☐ middle   ☐ end

2. The person who shared the videos did not worry about his privacy.   ☐ middle   ☐ end

3. She recently moved to a city which is very multicultural.   ☐ middle   ☐ end

4. The bilingual people who I know are all very successful.   ☐ middle   ☐ end

5. The information I found online doesn't seem correct.   ☐ middle   ☐ end

6. They became friends with somebody who lives in another country.   ☐ middle   ☐ end

E GRAMMAR Insert a caret (^) where you can add the adjective clause to each sentence. Write the letter of the adjective clause.

a. that anyone can learn

b. that are bicultural

c. that people joined in the 1980s

d. which developed 9,500 years ago

e. which was like Internet slang

f. who live in large cities

g. who speak two languages well

1. __d__ The urban areas ^ were villages and small towns.

2. _____ Studies show that many people can feel lonely.

3. _____ Becoming more open to other cultures is a skill.

4. _____ Members of CB radio communities used language.

5. _____ The online communities were not very advanced.

6. _____ The word "bilingual" describes people.

7. _____ People are often creative and open to new ideas.

F GRAMMAR Complete these sentences with an adjective clause. Use some subject clauses and some object clauses.

1. I enjoy talking to people _____.

2. Online communities _____ are my favorite kind.

3. In general, my friends are people _____.

4. In the future, I want to get a job _____.

5. People _____ usually reach their goals.

6. I never eat foods _____.

A grandmother has a video chat with her granddaughter.

G EDIT Read part of a student essay. Find and correct five errors with adjective clauses.

Online communities have some good points. For example, I use social media to stay in touch with family members and friends which I don't see very often. They are also a good way for people who have unusual hobbies to find other people who likes the same things. However, on the whole, I feel that virtual communities are bad, especially for people spend a lot of time online. Often the posts and photos who I see online only show people having fun and smiling. If people who are unhappy see these positive posts, they might feel worse. Another problem is that many people spend too much time using social media and other online communities. This means they cannot spend time doing things that they are more important, such as homework or being with family.

PLAN & WRITE

H BRAINSTORM Review the unit task, "Do you agree or disagree that joining online communities is good for teenagers?" Complete the chart with arguments for both sides. Include reasons and examples from this unit.

Online communities are good for teenagers.	
Agree	Disagree

WRITING TIP

When you brainstorm, start by thinking about the topic generally and then analyze your ideas to decide if they match the specific essay question. For this writing task, for example, first brainstorm ideas about whether online communities are good or bad for everyone. Then decide which of your ideas are relevant to teenagers.

I OUTLINE Look at the ideas that you brainstormed. Write an outline in your notebook by answering these questions.

Introductory paragraph

▶ Do you agree or disagree that joining online communities is good for young adults?

▶ What will your thesis statement be?

▶ What other information will you include?

Body paragraphs

▶ What two or three reasons will you give for your opinion?

▶ How will you support the main reason in each body paragraph?

Concluding paragraph

▶ How will you summarize your opinion?

▶ What final thought will you give about the topic?

J FIRST DRAFT Use your outline to write a first draft of your opinion essay.

K REVISE Use this list as you write your second draft.

☐ Does your essay have an introductory paragraph with background information and a thesis statement?

☐ Does it have two or three body paragraphs, each with a topic sentence and supporting ideas?

☐ Does each body paragraph show unity by focusing on just one idea?

☐ Does the essay have a conclusion that summarizes your opinion and reasons?

☐ Is there any information you could add to make your ideas clearer?

L EDIT Use this list as you write your final draft.

☐ Did you use adjective clauses correctly?

☐ Are there any spelling, word choice, punctuation, or grammar mistakes?

☐ Do the sentences vary in length and structure (e.g., some are longer, and some are shorter)?

M FINAL DRAFT Reread your final draft and correct any remaining errors. Then submit it to your teacher.

REFLECT

A Check (✓) the Reflect activities you can do and the academic skills you can use.

☐ rank reasons for joining online communities

☐ consider the value of being part of a community

☐ evaluate the benefits of multicultural cities

☐ compare the benefits of different communities

☐ write an opinion essay about online communities

☐ recognize how information is supported

☐ organize an opinion essay

☐ adjective clauses

☐ understand a writer's purpose

B Write the target words from the unit in the correct column. Add any other words that you learned. Circle words you still need to practice.

NOUN	VERB	ADJECTIVE	ADVERB & OTHER

C Reflect on the ideas in the unit as you answer these questions.

1. Did anything in this unit cause you to change how you feel about real or virtual communities?

_____

_____

2. What is the most important thing you learned in this unit?

_____

_____

CROSSING CULTURES

Schwartz's Deli, a well-known delicatessen, in Montreal, Canada

IN THIS UNIT

▸ Relate to different aspects of culture

▸ Evaluate opinions about culture

▸ Consider how culture can influence a brand

▸ Synthesize ideas about culture

▸ Write a descriptive essay about cultural symbols

SKILLS

READING
Understand unfamiliar vocabulary

WRITING
Add supporting ideas and details

GRAMMAR
The passive voice

CRITICAL THINKING
Evaluate the strength of an argument

CONNECT TO THE TOPIC

1. What aspects of culture does the photo show?
2. How do you think the title of the unit relates to the photo?

Watching a parade in Toronto, Canada

WHAT IS "CULTURE?"

A You are going to watch a video that answers the question "What is 'Culture?'" Cross out any ideas that you think the speakers will NOT mention.

1. The traditions, customs, and values of one group of people
2. The things that people from one place often eat or drink
3. The kinds of music and dance that are typical of one area
4. The types of machines and equipment that people often buy
5. The sports and games that people enjoy playing and watching
6. The art and architecture (such as buildings) from one place
7. The designs, colors, and shapes that are important in one area
8. The clothes that one group of people traditionally or often wear
9. The movies, television programs, and books that people like
10. The things that make people different or bring them together

B Compare your ideas from activity A with a partner. Then watch the video to check the answers. ▶ 2.1

C Discuss the questions in a small group.

1. Do you agree that all of the ideas from activity A are examples of culture? Why or why not?
2. Which ideas from activity A are the most important parts of culture for you? Why?

PREPARE TO READ

A VOCABULARY Read the paragraphs. Write the words in bold next to their definitions.

▶ Toronto and Montreal are both very **diverse** cities. Although English and French are Canada's two **official** languages, it's common to hear **multiple** languages on the streets of both cities.

▶ Some kinds of cooking combine flavors and styles from two or more places. Pacific Rim dishes **illustrate** this idea. Pacific Rim food is a **fusion** of cooking techniques and ingredients from the United States, Peru, Japan, and other **nations**.

▶ Stereotypes are common ideas about people from a specific country or group. These ideas are often negative, but they can be positive. For example, being on time and following the rules are positive **values**, and many people think these stereotypes **symbolize** people from Germany.

▶ Cultural globalization can **occur** when one society influences another through the Internet, food, or international travel. Rather than **divide** people, cultural globalization can bring them together.

1. _____ (adj) many

2. _____ (n) a country

3. _____ (v) to represent

4. _____ (v) to happen

5. _____ (v) to separate

6. _____ (adj) different

7. _____ (adj) decided by the government

8. _____ (n) beliefs about what is important in life

9. _____ (v) to give an example of; to show

10. _____ (n) a combination

B PERSONALIZE Discuss these questions with a partner.

1. What is the most **diverse nation** you know of or have visited?
2. Do you think social media **divides** people or brings them together?
3. Have you eaten any **fusion** food? What was it a fusion of?

REFLECT   Relate to different aspects of culture.

You are going to read an article about different parts of a culture. Write answers to these questions in your notebook. Then share your ideas and reasons in a small group.

1. What different aspects of culture (from the video) is your country most famous for?
2. What different aspects of culture are you most interested in?

READ

CULTURAL CONFUSION?

A PREDICT Read the title and first paragraph. Then skim the rest of the article by reading the first sentence of each paragraph. What do you think the article is about?

a. A comparison of ways that people from different cultures do things

b. A description of some of the ways that cultures influence each other

c. An explanation of how different cultures view food and music

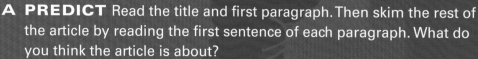

1   Like many abstract[1] ideas, culture is hard to define. A dictionary might describe it as the customs, **values**, arts, and way of life shared by people from a particular **nation** or group. This definition suggests culture is everything that makes one kind of people different from other kinds of people. On a certain level, this makes sense. After all, societies *do* differ from each other in obvious ways. However, when specific instances of culture are examined, it becomes clear that this definition misses an important point. Different cultures can be surprisingly similar because they often change and shape each other.

[1]**abstract** (adj) existing as an idea but not as a real thing

K-pop band BTS performing in Los Angeles, California, USA

2   Food is such an important part of culture that certain dishes have come to **symbolize** particular cultures. Apple pie, for instance, is closely linked with the United States. In fact, "as American as apple pie" is a familiar expression to describe something typical of U.S. culture. However, this classic dish is actually a **fusion** of elements from different regions. The top and bottom of the pie are made from wheat, which is originally from the Middle East. The filling[2] is made from apples, which are originally from Central Asia, sugar from India, and cinnamon from Asia. Surprisingly, not even the recipe is American. The first recorded description of how to make apple pie comes from England and dates from 1381.

3   Music can represent cultures, too. J-pop and K-pop, for example, are well known around the world as symbols of Japan and Korea. Like the example of apple pie, these musical genres have been influenced by other cultures. J-pop combines elements of traditional Japanese music with rock and dance music from Western countries. The influences on K-pop are even more **diverse** than those of J-pop. K-pop has been described as a fusion of traditional Korean music with **multiple** other styles, including rock, jazz, gospel, hip-hop, reggae, country, and even classical music.

4   It's not surprising that food and music can be a fusion of ideas and styles from different cultures, but what about languages? Does a language represent just the culture of its speakers? Because all languages have been influenced by other languages over a long period, the short answer is no. Take the example of modern English. About one-quarter of its words come from Old English, the earliest recorded form of the English language. The rest come from Latin and French (roughly 30 percent each), Greek (approximately 6 percent), and other sources (about 9 percent). English is somewhat unusual because it has been affected by so many other tongues, but every language has loan words that have been "borrowed" from other languages. *Anime* is an interesting example. Japanese speakers borrowed it from the English word *animation* to describe any kind of animated TV show or movie. Later, English speakers borrowed it back to describe animations that are typical of Japanese culture.

5   The writer George Bernard Shaw once joked that Britain and America are two cultures **divided** by the same language. In fact, the opposite is often true: Cultures that share the same language change each other. For example, Brazilian vloggers[3] are popular among young people in Portugal; as a result, some young Portuguese people are now speaking and dressing more like Brazilians. In addition, the **official** spelling of Portuguese words now follows Brazilian standards. Other examples of this kind of cultural influence can be found among the many countries where people speak English, Spanish, Arabic, or other global languages.

6   While culture can be defined as everything that makes one group of people different from other groups, it is much more than this. As the examples above **illustrate**, culture is also a fusion of flavors, styles, ideas, and words from different peoples and different places. Cultural fusion has been **occurring** for thousands of years, and will certainly continue as our world becomes ever more globally connected.

---

[2]**filling** (n) the layer of food inside a pie or sandwich

[3]**vlogger** (n) a person who makes or uploads video blogs

B MAIN IDEAS Check (✓) the two statements that summarize the main ideas. Incorrect answers either summarize less important ideas or are ideas that are not in the article.

1. _____ People from different countries may have different ways to define culture.

2. _____ Things such as food, music, and language can be symbols of a particular culture.

3. _____ Cultures can influence each other in different ways.

4. _____ The recipe for apple pie has been influenced by many cultures.

5. _____ Portuguese, English, Spanish, and Arabic are all spoken in multiple countries.

C DETAILS Use phrases from the article to complete the statements.

a shared language	about one-quarter	different cultures	multiple other styles
none of its ingredients	thousands of years		

1. Although it's clear that _____ vary in many ways, it's also true that they can influence one another.

2. Apple pie is a symbol of the United States, but the recipe is actually from England and _____ are originally from the U.S.

3. K-pop is a popular style of music and is a fusion of elements of traditional Korean music with _____.

4. _____ of the words in modern English originally come from Old English. The rest are from other languages.

5. Countries that have _____, such as Brazil and Portugal, can influence each other's cultures.

6. The process of cultural fusion has been going on for _____ and will almost certainly continue.

READING SKILL Understand unfamiliar vocabulary

When you read a text, you may see words that you don't know. In some cases, clues from context—other words around the unfamiliar one—can help you. In other cases, you can use clues in the word itself, such as how it is spelled.

For example, in paragraph 1, you can guess that *differ* probably means *to be different* because of the context. You might also notice the spellings of *differ* and *different* are similar.

*This definition suggests culture is everything that makes one kind of people different from other kinds of people. On a certain level, this makes sense. After all, societies do **differ** from each other in obvious ways.*

D APPLY Look for context clues for these words. Circle the correct definition. With a partner, discuss which context clues helped you find the definition.

1. **instances** (paragraph 1)   decisions / examples / opinions
2. **shape** (paragraph 1)   experience / influence / introduce
3. **classic** (paragraph 2)   delicious and healthy / new but well liked / popular and well known
4. **regions** (paragraph 2)   countries or large areas / foods or ingredients / long periods of time
5. **originally** (paragraph 2)   in the beginning / right now / a little later

E APPLY Find these words in paragraphs 3 and 4 and discuss what you think they mean with a partner. Write your definitions in your notebook.

genres   elements   somewhat   sources   tongues

REFLECT   Evaluate opinions about culture.

In your notebook, say whether you agree or disagree with these opinions about culture. Give reasons and examples. Then compare your ideas with a partner.

1. Music can represent culture.
2. Two cultures can be divided by the same language.
3. Cultural fusion will continue in the future.

Jalan Alor market,
Kuala Lumpur, Malaysia

PREPARE TO READ

A VOCABULARY Read the paragraph. Then choose the correct definition for each word.

One U.S. company hoped to **profit** when it began **trading** with businesses in Asia and the Middle East. Unfortunately, the name of one of the company's **brands** gave some people in those regions a negative **impression**. The company was **criticized** on social media, so it decided to change that name. The woman who **founded** the company apologized and said her company **respected** everyone. She also **announced** a plan to develop **guidelines** to help the company be more **sensitive** in the future.

1. **profit** (v)   a. to make a difficult choice   b. to earn money or a benefit
2. **trade** (v)   a. to buy and sell things   b. to move to a new place
3. **brand** (n)   a. a way to do business   b. a type of product made by a company
4. **impression** (n)   a. an event or experience   b. an opinion or idea
5. **criticize** (v)   a. to stop doing something   b. to say negative things about something
6. **found** (v)   a. to start a company   b. to look for something
7. **respect** (v)   a. to communicate with   b. to treat as important
8. **announce** (v)   a. to say something officially   b. to worry about something
9. **guideline** (n)   a. a product to sell   b. a rule to follow
10. **sensitive** (adj)   a. angry about new ideas   b. careful of others' feelings

B PERSONALIZE Discuss these questions in a small group.

1. What **brands** or products do you have a positive **impression** of?
2. Are there any companies or **brands** you have **criticized** in the past? Explain.
3. How can you show **respect** for and be **sensitive** to other cultures? Explain.
4. What **guidelines** do you have to follow at school?

REFLECT   Consider how culture can influence a brand.

You are going to read an article about brand names. Match these brands to the places they are from. Does the brand name give you a positive, negative, or neutral feeling about that culture? Discuss in a small group.

Brands
1. _____ 7-Eleven
2. _____ Amazon
3. _____ Lego
4. _____ Emirates Airlines
5. _____ Red Bull
6. _____ Samsung

Nations
a. Austria
b. Denmark
c. Japan
d. South Korea
e. the UAE
f. the USA

READ

WHAT'S IN A **NAME?**

A PREVIEW Scan the text. What brand names are mentioned? Which ones do you know?

🎧 2.2

1   Historically, societies have influenced each other in peaceful ways through sharing information and **trading** goods[1]. For centuries, this process was limited because travel across long distances was difficult, time consuming, and costly. As a result, most cultural influences happened between nearby nations and over a long period of time. Today, however, the Internet and international travel make it possible for ideas, people, and goods to spread easily and cheaply. As a result, the influence of one culture on another is occurring more rapidly than ever before—a trend known as cultural globalization.

---

[1]**goods** (n) things that people make in order to sell

An ice-cream shop in the Dubai International Airport, Dubai, United Arab Emirates

2   For businesses, cultural globalization offers the chance to sell products and provide services to new markets[2]. In order to **profit** from greater sales, however, it's increasingly important for companies to be **sensitive** to the needs and feelings of consumers in different cultures. This isn't always an easy thing to do. **Brand** and product names are a particular challenge that companies face when selling in the global marketplace.

3   In general, companies can follow simple **guidelines** when developing brand or product names that work across cultures. It's important to choose a name that's easy to read and pronounce in all of their target markets. It's also important to make sure that the name doesn't sound like a word with a negative meaning in the languages spoken in any of those markets. The name of the photography and electronics company *Kodak*, for example, was chosen because it was easy to say and had no negative meanings. In contrast, although the Japanese sports drink *Pocari Sweat*[3] is easy to say in English, its meaning is somewhat negative to people from English-speaking cultures.

4   In addition to following the commonsense guidelines for names, some companies use a strategy called "foreign branding." The basic idea is to choose

[2]**market** (n) a place to buy things or a group of people that might buy something

[3]**sweat** (n) liquid that comes from your skin when you exercise or are hot

a name that sounds like it comes from a culture that customers feel positively about. For example, *Giordano* may sound Italian, but this fashion company is from Hong Kong. The founder, Jimmy Lai, chose the name because he thought customers would react positively to Italian fashion. Ice cream brand *Häagen-Dazs* is supposed to look and sound Danish, but the term has no meaning in any language. The American who **founded** the company chose the name because he felt customers generally had a good **impression** of Denmark. And starting in the 1980s, the British retail chain[4] *Currys* sold products under the *Matsui* brand because that name sounded Japanese, and shoppers in the U.K. had a high opinion of electronic goods from Japan.

5   Foreign branding doesn't always work out. For instance, a well-known American businesswoman **announced** that she had created a fashion brand called *Kimono*. She chose this name because she loved and **respected** Japanese culture and felt her customers would feel the same. However, just six days later she announced an alternative name: *Skims*. Why the sudden change? A kimono—her original choice—is a traditional item of Japanese clothing. People all over the world **criticized** the businesswoman for cultural appropriation: that is, for trying to profit from something important to another culture. Daisaku Kadokawa, the mayor of Kyoto, a major Japanese city, even wrote to her to explain that kimonos are not a fashion symbol but are a symbol of the "beauty, spirit, and values of the Japanese" people.

6   Cultural globalization is likely to become an even more important phenomenon. As a result, choosing culturally appropriate and globally appealing names is also likely to become more important. The next time you're deciding which brand to buy, ask yourself how much brand names might affect your decision.

---

[4]**retail chain** (n) a group of shops controlled by one company

Women wearing traditional kimonos take selfies on the observatory of one of Japan's tallest buildings, Osaka, Japan.

B MAIN IDEAS Match the paragraph number (2–5) with its main idea. One idea is extra.

a. _____ Foreign branding involves choosing a brand name that sounds like it comes from a culture that customers view positively.

b. _____ If customers feel a brand name does not respect the original culture, they may see the name as cultural appropriation.

c. _____ In theory, cultural globalization can benefit companies, but in practice, it creates certain challenges.

d. _____ In the past, shoppers in the U.K. and Europe had a positive impression of electronics that were made in Japan.

e. _____ There are easy-to-understand rules that companies can follow when they want to choose an effective brand name.

C DETAILS In your notebook, write answers to the questions.

1. What two things are causing cultural globalization to happen faster?

2. Why is it important for companies to be sensitive to the feelings of consumers from multiple cultures?

3. What two guidelines should companies follow when choosing a name for their brand or product?

4. Why did a Hong Kong clothing company choose a brand name that sounds Italian?

5. Why did customers criticize a U.S. businesswoman's first choice of brand name?

D Reread paragraphs 1 and 2 and find the words or phrases with these meanings.

1. _____ (adj) without violence or a fight

2. _____ (adj) taking a long time to do

3. _____ (adj) expensive

4. _____ (adj) quickly

5. _____ (v) to experience

E Find and underline these words in the reading. Write definitions and discuss your ideas with a partner.

1. strategy (paragraph 4) _____

2. founder (paragraph 4) _____

3. alternative (paragraph 5) _____

4. appealing (paragraph 6) _____

CRITICAL THINKING   Evaluate the strength of an argument

When you evaluate an argument, you read it carefully and consider how convincing the writer's ideas are. Evaluating is different from criticizing. Criticizing usually focuses on negative things, but evaluating may focus either on positive or negative things. When you evaluate an argument or opinion, ask yourself questions such as *How well does the writer make his or her point?* or *How could the writer's argument be improved?*

F   APPLY Choose the correct answers. Then discuss your answers in a small group.

1. What is the writer's overall argument or thesis?

    a. The influence of one culture on another is occurring more rapidly than ever before—a trend known as cultural globalization.

    b. Brand and product names are a particular challenge that companies face when selling in the global marketplace.

2. Which added information would improve paragraph 1 of the article?

    a. An explanation of how the Internet was invented

    b. An example of peaceful cultural influence

3. How does the writer make the argument in paragraph 3 more effective?

    a. By giving examples that illustrate the point

    b. By including statistics that support the point

4. Which added information would improve paragraph 4?

    a. Statistics that show how successful foreign branding can be

    b. An example of foreign branding from the hotel industry

5. What could be cut from paragraph 5 without affecting the writer's point?

    a. The explanation of why the American businesswoman chose *Kimono* originally

    b. The information about what Daisaku Kadokawa wrote in his letter

REFLECT   Synthesize ideas about culture.

"Synthesize" means to put ideas from different sources together. This helps you look at a topic in a new way. Think about the articles that you have read in this unit. Make notes to answer the questions. Then compare your ideas in a small group.

1. What are some points about culture that both articles mention?

2. What are some points about culture that only one article mentions?

3. Are there any points about culture that the two articles disagree on?

4. Which ideas give you a new perspective on culture?

WRITE

A Scottish bagpiper in traditional clothing

Write a descriptive essay about cultural symbols.

You are going to write an essay that describes two things that are important symbols of your culture. Use the ideas, vocabulary, and skills from the unit.

A MODEL Read the descriptive essay. Underline the thesis statement and the topic sentences for the two body paragraphs.

Two Important Cultural Symbols

Scotland has a long history, and in my view, there are many things that symbolize Scottish culture. These include art and design, literature and language, and food and drink. However, I believe that kilts and bagpipes are the two most important symbols of Scotland.

The kilt is a traditional skirt from Scotland. Scottish people have been wearing kilts for a long time. In fact, kilts were first worn several hundred years ago. Kilts are made from wool and have a pattern of stripes called "tartan." In the past, only men wore kilts. These days, women sometimes wear them, but men still wear them more often. In general, kilts are common for special events such as weddings, festivals, or sports competitions, but they can be worn every day. Some people in Ireland have a tradition of wearing kilts, too. However, the kilt is a more important symbol for Scotland because even people from other countries recognize it as Scottish.

The bagpipe is a traditional musical instrument from Scotland. A bagpipe has two main parts: a bag and some pipes. Air is blown into the bag through one pipe. When the bag is full, the air comes out through the other pipes and makes a sound. Scottish people have played bagpipes for hundreds of years. There is evidence that they were introduced to Scotland 600 or more years ago. These days, bagpipe music can be heard at funerals, weddings, and other special events.

In conclusion, kilts and bagpipes are important symbols of Scotland because they are easily recognized as being Scottish. In addition, some people whose families came from Scotland in the past still wear kilts or play bagpipes as a way to remember their original culture.

B ANALYZE THE MODEL Number these questions (1–6) in the order they are answered in paragraph 2 of the model essay.

a. _____ What are kilts made from, and what do they look like?

b. _____ What are kilts?

c. _____ When did people first wear kilts?

d. _____ When or how often do people wear kilts now?

e. _____ Who wears kilts?

f. _____ Why are kilts an important symbol of Scotland?

C ANALYZE THE MODEL In your notebook, write the questions that are answered in paragraph 3 of the model essay. Then compare your ideas with a partner.

WRITING SKILL   Add supporting ideas and details

When you write an essay, it's important to include specific information that supports your main ideas and opinions. One way to do this is to answer questions readers might have. For example, a reader might want to ask *when* something was invented, *who* first had an idea, *where* something occurred, *how often* an event happened, or *why* something is important.

Using the answers to questions to add supporting information can help you stay on topic and make sure each idea belongs in the paragraph. This is important to help you write paragraphs with unity.

D APPLY Use the notes below to add sentences with supporting information to the beginning of this paragraph. Write in your notebook.

Although it is not a famous sport, kabaddi is popular in some countries. For instance, it is the national sport in Bangladesh and is popular in India and Pakistan, too.

Where popular?	Bangladesh (national sport), India, Pakistan
Where play?	outside (traditional)/inside (common)
How to play?	2 teams with 7 players
How to score?	touch players on other team to get points
How to win?	get more points than other team

GRAMMAR   The passive voice

English verbs have two voices: **active** and **passive**.

▸ Use the **active voice** to focus on the person or thing that *does* the action, or **agent**.

▸ Use the **passive voice** to focus on the person or thing the action *happens to*, or **receiver**.

To form the passive, use *be* + the past participle of the main verb. The form (present, past, etc.) of the verb is shown in *be*.

Active   <u>Sushi chefs</u> **make** <u>sushi</u> with raw fish and rice.
           subject (agent)   object (receiver)

Passive   <u>Sushi</u> **is made** with raw fish and rice.
           subject (receiver)

The passive voice is common in academic and formal writing. The agent is often not included, but is sometimes added after *by*:

Sushi is originally from Japan, but it is now enjoyed **by people all over the world**.

U Mumba and the Gujarat Fortune Giants compete during a Pro Kabaddi League match in Jaipur, Rajasthan, India.

E GRAMMAR Find and write these examples of passive forms from the model essay.

1. Three examples of simple present verbs in the passive voice:

   Kilts are made _____ _____

   _____

2. Two examples of simple past verbs in the passive voice:

   _____ _____

3. Two examples of the modal *can* in the passive voice:

   _____ _____

F GRAMMAR Complete these sentences with the passive form of the verbs in parentheses.

1. Pizza is originally from Italy, but now it _____ (eat) all over the world.

2. *Noh* is a type of theater performance. It can _____ (see) throughout Japan.

3. Arabic _____ (speak) in many Middle Eastern countries, such as Oman.

4. Music from traditional instruments such as the *erhu* and *dizi* can _____ (hear) in China.

5. The stone pyramids of Egypt and Mexico _____ (build) a very long time ago.

6. One traditional item of clothing worn in South Korea _____ (call) a *hanbok*.

7. A popular South American drink _____ (make) from *yerba mate* leaves.

8. Baseball _____ (invent) in the United States, but today it _____ (play) in many places.

G GRAMMAR Discuss these questions with a partner. Use passive voice when possible in your answers and write down what your partner says in your notebook.

1. What is a traditional food from your culture? How is it made? When is it usually eaten?

2. What is a traditional item of clothing from your culture? What is it made of? When is it usually worn?

3. What is an important building or monument in your country? When was it built? Why was it built?

4. What is a popular sport in your culture? How is it played? When and where is it played? Why is it popular?

Editing does not always involve finding and fixing grammar mistakes or spelling errors. Sometimes editing can involve improving your writing. For example, it might be good to change a sentence into the passive voice if the agent is not known, not important, or has already been mentioned.

H EDIT Read the paragraph. Find and correct five errors with the passive voice.

Feijoada is a symbol of Brazil. In fact, it sometimes called the Brazilian national dish even though it is also eaten in many other nations. The dish includes beans, meat, and sometimes vegetables. The color of the beans depends on where the dish made. In most parts of Brazil, black beans are use, but in some parts, *feijoada* can be made with brown or red beans. Traditionally, *feijoada* is cooked slowly in a clay pot over low heat. After it is ready, it usually served with white rice and slices of orange. In some parts of Brazil, the custom is to have *feijoada* on Wednesdays and Saturdays. In other parts of the country, it's traditionally eat on Fridays.

PLAN & WRITE

I BRAINSTORM Think about things that are important symbols of your culture. These could be kinds of food or drink, styles of music or dance, a type of art, an item of clothing, or even a sport. Complete the chart with your ideas.

An important symbol of my culture	Why is it important?	What questions would someone ask about it?

J OUTLINE Choose two symbols of your culture from activity I. Use the structure below to write an outline in your notebook.

Introductory paragraph

- ▶ Background information
- ▶ Thesis statement

Body paragraph 1

- ▶ Description of symbol
- ▶ Why it's important

Body paragraph 2

- ▶ Description of symbol
- ▶ Why it's important

Concluding paragraph

- ▶ Summary statement
- ▶ Final comment

K FIRST DRAFT Use your outline to write a first draft of your descriptive essay.

L REVISE Use this list as you write your second draft.

- ☐ Does your essay clearly describe two important symbols of your culture?
- ☐ Does your essay have an introductory paragraph with a clear thesis statement?
- ☐ Does it have two body paragraphs that answer questions readers may have about the symbols?
- ☐ Does the information in each body paragraph follow a logical order?
- ☐ Is there any information that is not needed?
- ☐ Does your concluding paragraph have a summary statement and a final comment?

M EDIT Use this list as you write your final draft.

- ☐ Does your essay use the passive voice correctly?
- ☐ Are there any spelling, word choice, punctuation, or grammar mistakes?
- ☐ Do the sentences vary in length and structure (e.g., some are longer, and some are shorter)?

N FINAL DRAFT Reread your final draft and correct any errors. Then submit it to your teacher.

REFLECT

A Check (✓) the Reflect activities you can do and the academic skills you can use.

- ☐ relate to different aspects of culture
- ☐ evaluate opinions about culture
- ☐ consider how culture influences a brand
- ☐ synthesize ideas about culture
- ☐ write a descriptive essay about cultural symbols

- ☐ understand unfamiliar vocabulary
- ☐ add supporting ideas and details
- ☐ the passive voice
- ☐ evaluate the strength of an argument

B Write the target words from the unit in the correct column. Add any other words that you learned. Circle words you still need to practice.

NOUN	VERB	ADJECTIVE	ADVERB & OTHER

C Reflect on the ideas in the unit as you answer these questions.

1. What topic from this unit would you like to know more about, and why?

_____

_____

2. What is the most important thing you learned in this unit?

_____

_____

PLAYING
WITH DESIGN

A climbing wall inside an office building, Cambridge, UK

IN THIS UNIT

▶ Consider the importance of play

▶ Relate ideas about play to your life

▶ Consider how design can change behavior

▶ Create a design to change behavior

▶ Write a description of a diagram

SKILLS

READING
Make inferences

WRITING
Describe a process

GRAMMAR
Noun modifiers

CRITICAL THINKING
Connect new ideas to what you know

CONNECT TO THE TOPIC

1. How does the photo relate to the title of the unit?
2. What aspects of design are you most interested in? Why?

47

WATCH RECYCLE

Plastic bags, cans, and milk containers at a recycling center, Nova Scotia, Canada

RETHINKING WASTE

A You are going to watch a video about two people who use plastic waste to help others. Complete these summaries with phrases from the box.

| 200 plastic bags | local area | nice colors | plastic string | recycled ones | six plastic bottles |

Tom Meades turns plastic waste into Bluetooth speakers. First, his company takes plastic waste from the [1]_____. Then they clean it and melt it down in an oven. After that, they twist the plastic to get [2]_____ and patterns. Finally, they put it in molds and press the molds together. When the speakers are cool, they pull the molds apart. In total, each speaker helps to recycle about [3]_____.

Dr. Karthikeyan Kandan turns plastic waste into prosthetic sockets[1] for people who have lost a leg. Each socket is made from [4]_____. First, he grinds the bottles into powder and then turns the powder into a kind of [5]_____ called "yarn." A machine knits the yarn into the right shape. Finally, the socket goes in an oven. Prosthetic sockets usually cost $3,000 to $6,000, but Dr. Kandan's [6]_____ can be made for $12 each.

[1]**prosthetic socket** (n phr) a way to connect an artificial arm or leg to a human body

B Watch the video to check your answers to activity A. ▶3.1

C **PERSONALIZE** Discuss the questions in a small group.

1. Which of the two processes do you think is more creative? Why?
2. If you started a company that used recycled plastic waste, what would you make, and why?

PREPARE TO READ

A VOCABULARY Read the sentences. Choose the definitions for the words in bold.

1. Organization, clarity, grammar, and mechanics are **elements** of good writing.

   a. parts
   b. ideas

2. Good managers **encourage** their team to share their ideas.

   a. to pay
   b. to push; motivate

3. Businesspeople often **exchange** business cards when they meet for the first time.

   a. to give something and get something in return
   b. to give something to please someone

4. Designers make **key** decisions about how things look and work.

   a. important
   b. difficult

5. Many people believe that it's possible to **overcome** problems with hard work.

   a. to solve or deal with
   b. to discuss or talk about

6. Designers need a **range** of skills, including being creative and listening effectively.

   a. small group
   b. variety

7. Scientists develop new medicines that help doctors **treat** serious diseases.

   a. to understand
   b. to cure

8. Summer clothes are usually light and cool, making them **unsuitable** for cold weather.

   a. not right
   b. not liked

9. Finding a job you care about is **vital** to being happy at work.

   a. necessary
   b. expensive

10. Helping people enjoy their lives more and feel happier is a **worthwhile** goal.

    a. taking a long time
    b. important or useful

B PERSONALIZE Make a list for three of the following topics. Then compare lists with a partner.

- ▶ **key** skills successful students have
- ▶ **worthwhile** goals for yourself this month
- ▶ problems you **overcame** with hard work
- ▶ words that can **encourage** other people

REFLECT Consider the importance of play.

You are going to read about using playful solutions to overcome problems. Work with a small group. Unscramble these opinions about play. Then discuss what each one means, and whether you agree or disagree with it and why.

for the unexpected / good training / play is

_____

play can help / stronger social relationships / us build

_____

from play, no matter / how old we are / our brains benefit

_____

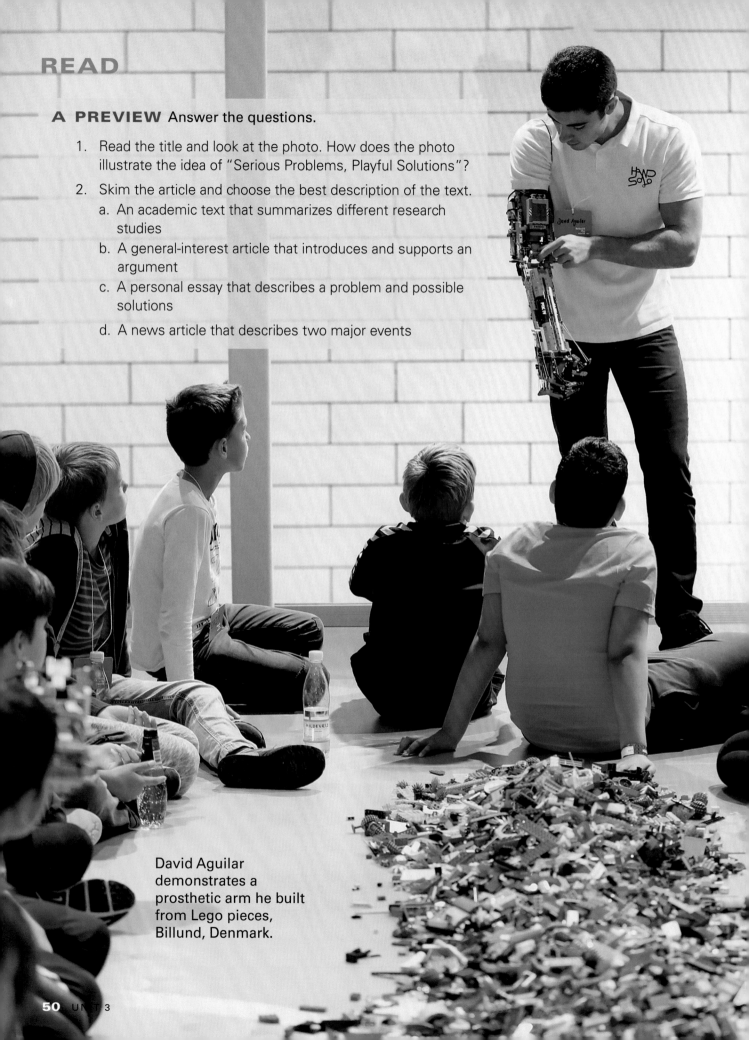

READ

A PREVIEW Answer the questions.

1. Read the title and look at the photo. How does the photo illustrate the idea of "Serious Problems, Playful Solutions"?

2. Skim the article and choose the best description of the text.
   a. An academic text that summarizes different research studies
   b. A general-interest article that introduces and supports an argument
   c. A personal essay that describes a problem and possible solutions
   d. A news article that describes two major events

David Aguilar demonstrates a prosthetic arm he built from Lego pieces, Billund, Denmark.

Forward to the Future

SERIOUS PROBLEMS,
PLAYFUL SOLUTIONS

🎧 3.1

1 When most people think of play, they think of something that children do. And it's true that play is **vital** for children: It helps them develop the physical and emotional skills they need for life. However, some experts argue that play has value for all ages because it helps us develop new ideas. When people play, they put things together in new ways and become aware of unexpected connections. Some designers and creators have put this theory into practice by using play to improve people's lives. This includes dealing with mental health issues, teaching useful skills and even protecting the environment.

2 One doesn't usually think of play when considering ways to help people with mental health issues. Traditional therapies and treatments have included a lot of talk and medicines. Recently, psychologists have started exploring more fun ways of helping these patients, for example, by using video games. Research shows that playing video games can have a positive effect on the brain and mood. Some game designers have taken this idea further. One example is SPARX, a video game that was designed to **treat** depression[1]. It teaches life skills to people who suffer from depression to help them deal with negative feelings and enjoy life. Other games have been designed to provide treatment for mental health issues such as PTSD[2] and ADHD[3]. For these kinds of patients, the type of game doesn't matter as much as the distraction it creates, the connection with other players, and the goal of the game. Video games hold the attention of people who find it challenging to concentrate in the rest of their lives.

3 Play may seem **unsuitable** for the workplace. However, it's actually becoming more common because companies have recognized that play can help workers develop **key** skills. Designers at global brands such as Lego and Playmobil have created special versions of their toys called Lego Serious Play and Playmobil Pro. Employees use these Lego bricks or Playmobil pieces to design models that show their ideas or plans. The models allow workers to see their ideas instead of just talk or write about them. They use toys to find new ways to develop solutions to problems. One user commented that she thought it was difficult to just start building something. By using play, she was able to allow herself to try, fail, and try again. When employees play in this way, they improve vital soft skills, such as effective communication, critical thinking, and creativity.

---

[1]**depression** (n) a mental illness that causes unhappiness

[2]**PTSD** (n) a mental illness caused by a stressful event

[3]**ADHD** (n) a condition that makes it hard for people to concentrate

4   Evidence suggests that play holds many benefits for education, as well. Finland is a small country, but when it comes to educational success, it's among the biggest in the world. A key reason for this success is that Finland's curriculum[4] for younger learners focuses on play. Instead of having children sit still in class, educators in Finland **encourage** them to play and move around. Although the children may not appear to be learning directly, playing actively helps them develop their ability to use language, understand math, and interact with others effectively. In addition, children build many of the same soft skills that are so valuable later in the workplace. The results of Finland's approach have been so effective that other nations have begun to copy it.

5   Because people of all ages love to play games, gamification has become an important concept in design and in a **range** of other fields over the last 10 to 15 years. In simple terms, gamification involves using **elements** of play, such as giving points, to make things more enjoyable and motivating. It's not just about having fun, though. Designers can use gamification to help solve issues affecting society. For example, a U.S.-based company called Recyclebank has designed a "gaming for good" membership program. In places where the program is available, people can join and earn points every time they take an action that benefits the planet, such as recycling. And those points have value. Members can save them up and **exchange** them for games and other rewards.

6   A dictionary might define *play* as using toys or games for fun. That sounds like the opposite of anything serious such as work. However, as the examples above show, play is **worthwhile** for everyone and in many situations. It encourages the young and not-so-young to think differently, to keep their minds open to new discoveries, and even helps to **overcome** some of the challenges of everyday life.

---

[4]**curriculum** (n) the subjects studied at a school or college

B MAIN IDEAS Complete the main ideas with the phrases. Two are extra. Then number the ideas in the order they appear in the article (1–6).

a success for children in Finland	one of the key benefits of play
both employers and employees	people with mental health issues
effective ideas for saving money	recycling and other behaviors
either new ideas or familiar ones	value for people of every age

a. _____ The fact that it lets people find solutions to life's challenges is

_____.

b. _____ Experts think that play has _____
and is not just for children.

c. _____ Gamification can encourage _____
that help the environment.

d. _____ Play can benefit _____ because it
builds key work skills.

e. _____ Play-based learning has been _____.

f. _____ Playing video games can benefit _____
such as depression.

C DETAILS Which types of design are discussed in the article? Write the number of the paragraph in which the type of design is discussed. Two choices are extra.

a. _____ Curriculum design

b. _____ Gamified design

c. _____ Graphic design

d. _____ Toy design

e. _____ Video game design

f. _____ Website design

D DETAILS Number the details from paragraph 5 in the correct order (1–4). Two details are extra.

a. _____ As members, they get points for each environmentally friendly action.

b. _____ In order to get more points, they continue doing beneficial things.

c. _____ Most members save points for 10–15 years to exchange for rewards.

d. _____ People choose to join Recyclebank's "gaming for good" program.

e. _____ There are many fun rewards, including toys and books for kids.

f. _____ They exchange points for rewards when they have enough of them.

READING SKILL Make inferences

When you make an inference, you use clues to understand something that is not stated directly in a text. In other words, you reach a conclusion based on ideas in the text and your own experience. For example, the text says, "_Some_ experts argue that play has value for all ages." From this, you can infer that not everyone believes play benefits people of all ages.

E APPLY Write *I* if you can infer the information from the reading. Write *NI* if you can't. Look for support in the paragraphs in parentheses. Then compare your ideas with a partner.

1. _____ Adults who play a lot have fewer problems than adults who play less. (paragraph 1)

2. _____ Traditional therapies for mental illness do not work. (paragraph 2)

3. _____ Some people with depression do not enjoy their lives very much. (paragraph 2)

4. _____ Lego Serious Play is more popular with companies than Playmobil Pro. (paragraph 3)

5. _____ Finland has different education systems for younger and older kids. (paragraph 4)

6. _____ Gamification is a new idea that was invented just 10 years ago. (paragraph 5)

7. _____ Recyclebank's program is not available in every part of the United States. (paragraph 5)

8. _____ Although playing is a physical activity, it can bring mental benefits. (paragraph 6)

Adults playing in a ball pit that contains 81,000 white balls, London, England

Answer these questions. Then discuss your ideas with a partner.

1. Do you think play could help you improve your life or deal with problems? Explain.

    _____

    _____

2. Will you try to include more play in your life after reading the article? If so, what kinds?

    _____

    _____

3. Check (✓) the three most important ways that play might help you.

    ☐ improve creativity   ☐ improve energy level

    ☐ develop social skills   ☐ enhance learning

    ☐ improve relationships   ☐ help solve problems

    ☐ increase happiness   ☐ improve communication

    ☐ reduce stress   ☐ raise fitness level

PREPARE TO READ

A VOCABULARY Match the beginning and ending of each definition.

1. A **figure** is the general shape of a _____
2. **Explicit** instructions _____
3. Products with an **appealing** design _____
4. Something **amusing**, such as a joke _____
5. A **cycle** is a series of actions or _____
6. The **proportion** of people who do _____
7. To **opt** to do something means to _____
8. To **promote** something means to _____
9. To **purchase**, or buy, means to spend _____
10. To **state** something means to write or _____

a. are attractive.
b. events that happen again and again.
c. encourage people to do it or buy it.
d. are clear and direct.
e. something is how many do it.
f. money to get something.
g. choose to do it.
h. or story, is funny and entertaining.
i. person or object.
j. say it in a clear, careful way.

B PERSONALIZE Discuss these questions with a partner.

1. Think about something you recently **purchased**. What did you buy, and why?
2. Think about something **amusing** that happened to you recently. Why was it funny?
3. Think of an **appealing** design. What makes it **appealing** to you?

REFLECT Consider how design can change behavior.

You are going to read about how design can influence actions and behavior. Choose the correct action word for each photo. Then discuss these questions in a small group.

1. How does the design of the object help you understand what to do?
2. How could you change the design of each object to make people do the opposite action?

start / stop

open / close

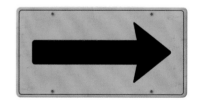

go / wait

THE POWER OF A NUDGE

A PREVIEW Work with a small group. Look at the photo and discuss the questions.

1. What does this design try to get people to do, and why?
2. How effective do you think it is, and why?

🎧 3.2

1   Look around you. Everything you see and use, whether it's a chair or an electronic device, has been designed by someone. Sometimes the most successful designs are the least obvious. Simple design changes can have a big impact on how we behave. One example is using play and gamification to make things more **appealing** and help us overcome challenges and problems. Another effective approach is an idea called *nudge theory*.

2   A nudge is a gentle push, with the type of push depending on the situation. Sometimes it's a physical push. A person might nudge a friend to make him move out of the way, or a parent might nudge a child to get her to say thank you for a gift. Sometimes a nudge is a mental push. A manager might nudge employees to work faster by reminding them that a deadline is coming up. In design terms, nudges usually have two characteristics. First, they make one choice or action seem more attractive or beneficial than other options. And second, design nudges suggest or imply the best option instead of being **explicit** about it.

3   An experiment in Lisbon, Portugal, provides a good example of a design nudge. The experiment was designed to make crossing the street safer. Instead of waiting for the walk signal, pedestrians were crossing whenever there was a break in traffic, which can be very dangerous. As part of the experiment, the usual walk signal was replaced. Instead of a standing **figure**, it showed a person dancing. This design nudge did not explicitly **state** that people should wait until the signal changed, but it gave them something **amusing** to watch— the dancing figure—and encouraged them to wait before crossing. As a result, the **proportion** of people who crossed at an unsafe time dropped significantly.

A three-dimensional crosswalk painted on a street, Schmalkalden, Germany

4   There are other examples of nudges designed to **promote** beneficial choices. Students can be nudged to replace a **cycle** of negative behavior—such as choosing unhealthy food at lunch—with positive behaviors. Studies show that the majority of people take the first three foods they see more often than other foods. Schools can use this information to nudge students to eat better by putting healthier food choices at the front of the line, and unhealthy ones at the end. More appealing food names can also affect student choices: "Crunchy summer salad" will probably be more popular than just "salad."

5   People don't notice when an effective design nudge pushes them toward a certain action or decision. For example, shining a light on fruit can increase sales, but putting a mirror behind doughnuts has the opposite effect. As a result, companies may develop nudges that benefit themselves, not consumers. A hotel that offers a free breakfast might **opt** to put low-cost but unhealthy items in a noticeable place and place higher cost but healthier items in a far corner. This helps the hotel save money but is less beneficial for guests. In-store sales are another example. Companies might advertise "Two for just $10" in very large letters to suggest this is a special price and so nudge people to **purchase** two, when in fact, the usual price—as shown in much smaller letters—is $5 each.

6   Design nudges are all around us because, like playful design, they are an effective way for designers to promote certain behaviors. Nudges are not just for designers, though. A growing number of people are finding that they can use nudges on themselves to help overcome problems and make better choices.

B MAIN IDEAS Check (✓) the four statements that summarize the main ideas. The other statements either summarize minor points or describe ideas the writer does not mention.

1. ☐ Everything around you has been designed by someone.
2. ☐ Nudges that change behavior can be either physical or mental.
3. ☐ Design nudges promote actions or choices by making them more attractive.
4. ☐ The dancing wait signal was an effective nudge because it made waiting fun.
5. ☐ People may not notice nudges because nudges suggest what to do rather than stating it.
6. ☐ Companies can benefit from design nudges that change how customers act.
7. ☐ Hotels that offer free breakfasts can save money by only offering a few foods.
8. ☐ Signs in stores can encourage customers to purchase more than they need.

C DETAILS Work with a partner. Look at the four statements you did not check in activity B. Which one(s) are less important points or details, and which one(s) are not mentioned in the article?

D DETAILS Write the number of the paragraph(s) where the author . . .

a. _____ describes the two features of typical design nudges.

b. _____ discusses some examples of design nudges in schools.

c. _____ explains how a design nudge improved safety in a city.

d. _____ introduces the idea that nudges can be bad for people.

e. _____ mentions nudges that may affect the foods people choose.

f. _____ refers to a nudge that might change how shoppers act.

E Complete the sentences with information from the reading.

1. Most people enjoy play and games. We can infer this because the text says that play and gamification ___*make things more appealing.*___.

2. Some _____ only have one of the two common characteristics.

   We can infer this because the article says they usually have both characteristics, not that they always do.

3. After the experiment in Lisbon ended, the proportion of people who _____ probably increased. We can infer this because they no longer had anything interesting to look at while waiting.

4. Fewer people choose to purchase doughnuts when there is a _____ them. We can infer this because doing so makes the doughnuts seem less appealing for some reason.

CRITICAL THINKING   Connect new ideas to what you know

When you learn new information, you can understand it better by connecting it to what you already know. It might be information you've read or situations you've experienced. For example, as you read about nudges and how they affect consumers, you might think about signs you've seen in stores that encourage shoppers to purchase several items. You can also consider whether those signs made you purchase more.

F   APPLY Discuss the questions in a small group.

1. Which of these examples from the article *Serious Problems, Playful Solutions* is a design nudge?

   a. Video games that treat mental health issues

   b. A gamified program that encourages recycling

   c. Toys that teach businesspeople soft skills

2. What design nudges have you experienced in your daily life? How effective are they?

REFLECT   Create a design to change behavior.

Work with a small group. Choose option 1, 2, or 3 and design, describe, or illustrate it. Then compare your ideas as a class. Which designs do you think are the best, and why?

1. A nudge that makes people think about others before they move their airplane seat back

2. A nudge that reminds office workers that looking at screens too much is bad for their eyes

3. A nudge that encourages people to waste less water in the bathroom or kitchen

WRITE

You are going to write a description of a process illustrated in a diagram. You will describe each step shown in the diagram. Use the ideas, vocabulary, and skills from the unit.

A MODEL Study the diagram and read the model description. Then choose the statement that best describes what "cradle-to-cradle design" is.

a. A way of making products that requires a lot of resources because the products are thrown away after they are used

b. A way to reduce the amount of waste that people produce by reusing some products and recycling other products

c. A way of designing products that helps the planet because old products are used to produce materials for making new ones

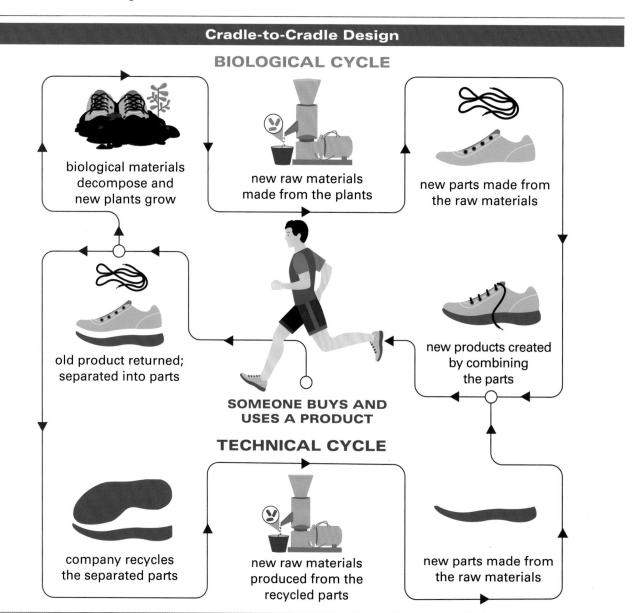

Cradle-to-Cradle Design

BIOLOGICAL CYCLE

biological materials decompose and new plants grow

new raw materials made from the plants

new parts made from the raw materials

old product returned; separated into parts

new products created by combining the parts

SOMEONE BUYS AND USES A PRODUCT

TECHNICAL CYCLE

company recycles the separated parts

new raw materials produced from the recycled parts

new parts made from the raw materials

The Cradle-to-Cradle Design Process

1   The cradle-to-cradle design process has two connected cycles: a biological cycle and a technical cycle. The biological cycle involves making things from wood or plants, such as cotton. The technical cycle involves making things from materials such as metal or plastic.

2   The process begins when a company makes a new product that includes biological and technical parts. The products, such as running shoes, go to stores, and they are purchased by customers. After someone has finished using the product, it goes back to the manufacturer. It's then separated into biological and technical parts.

3   In the technical cycle, the company recycles old materials to produce new raw materials. After that, these materials go to a factory. Workers at the factory make the raw materials into new parts, such as the plastic parts of a pair of running shoes.

4   In the biological cycle, plant materials decompose, or break down. This helps new plants grow. Then new raw materials are made from the plants. When the new materials are ready, they go to a factory. At the factory, those materials are turned into new parts, such as the upper parts of a pair of running shoes.

5   Finally, when the new product is ready, someone buys it and the cycle starts again.

WRITING SKILL   Describe a process

There are several important things to remember when you describe a process:

▸ Write an introduction that gives a general overview of the process.
▸ Describe, summarize, or explain each step in the order it happens.
▸ Use connecting words and adverb clauses so the order of the steps is clear: for example, *when the process begins*, *after that*, *finally*, etc.
▸ The passive voice in the simple present is common when describing a process.

There are also things you should avoid:

▸ You do not need a conclusion that summarizes the process.
▸ In general, you do not need to include any personal opinions.

B ANALYZE THE MODEL Answer the questions and find the examples in the model.

1. Which paragraphs give a summary of the biological cycle? _____ _____

2. Which paragraphs give a summary of the technical cycle? _____ _____

3. Which paragraph gives an overview of the process? _____

4. Find three examples of the passive voice.

    _____

    _____

    _____

5. Find three examples of connecting words or adverb clauses.

    _____

    _____

    _____

C Write the paragraph number where each statement could be added.

a. _____ Buyers then use the products in their daily lives.
b. _____ In total, the whole process has nine stages.
c. _____ Like in the technical cycle, these parts are used to make new finished products.
d. _____ These parts are used to manufacture new finished products.

WRITING TIP

A description is a type of analysis. When you write a description of a process, you analyze and explain the links between steps. You synthesize, or pull together, the steps so that your reader recognizes them and understands their place in the process.

Designing
boxes for toys,
North Andover,
Massachusetts, USA

GRAMMAR   Noun modifiers

You can add one or more modifiers to a noun to describe or give more information about it. Modifying nouns is common in academic English and can make your writing more natural and interesting. There are several ways to modify nouns.

Before the noun:

▶ with one or more adjectives   **new** shoes / **nice but expensive** shoes

▶ with -*ing* or -*ed* adjectives   an **exciting** movie / a **delayed** movie
   (formed from verbs)

▶ with another noun   a **job** interview / a **sports** interview

Notes: Adjectives and nouns that modify other nouns are never plural. However, nouns that
        always end with -*s* may look plural (***news*** *story,* ***economics*** *book*).
        If the noun phrase includes *a* or *an*, the article goes with the modifier, not with the noun
        (***an open*** *book*).

After the noun:

▶ with a linking verb and adjective / adjectives   Her idea **is obvious**.
                                   These ideas **are simple but helpful**.

▶ with a prepositional phrase   books **about history**
                                   a book **with a blue cover**

D GRAMMAR Underline the noun and circle the modifier(s) in each sentence.

1. This <u>book</u> is ⟨difficult but interesting⟩.

2. It's an exciting movie about robots.

3. These running shoes are expensive.

4. She is a fantastic math teacher.

5. We're having a surprise party for Ryan.

E GRAMMAR Put the words in parentheses in the most natural order to complete the sentences.

1. The _____. (design / is easy / process / to follow)

2. He's a _____. (designer / graphic / in / San Diego)

3. My _____. (amazing / but expensive / new / phone is)

4. Our _____. (manager / friendly / office / is usually very)

5. The _____. (art / closed / in town is / museum / today).

EDITING TIP

It is not common to use many short, simple sentences in academic writing. Noun modifiers allow you to join short ideas to make one longer sentence. For example, instead of "*The store has windows. The windows are large. The windows are for display.*" you can write "*The store has large display windows.*"

F EDIT Read this description of a process. Correct the five bold noun modifier errors.

Typical **designed processes** have four separate stages. In the first stage, designers think about the needs of a wide **variety users**. After this, they brainstorm and analyze many possible ideas. The third stage of the process involves designing and developing the idea from the second stage that is the best. When this stage is finished and the design is nearly final, the designers usually ask **a experienced** group of users for opinions and suggestions about the design. If necessary, the designers then repeat some earlier stages of the process in order to improve their **design final**. Following a design process like this one may not seem very **excite**, but it is important to make sure that the quality of the final product is good.

A design studio

PLAN & WRITE

For some writing tasks, such as describing a diagram or summarizing a text, you don't need to brainstorm ideas to include in your writing. Before you start writing, however, you will need to think about the best ways to describe or summarize the information and the best order in which to do this.

G You are going to write a description of the process outlined in the diagram below. Look at the diagram, and answer these questions.

1. What is the main point of the diagram? _____

_____

2. How many steps does the diagram include? _____

_____

3. Which steps do you need to include in your description? _____

_____

4. In what order should you describe them? _____

_____

Stages of a Design Process

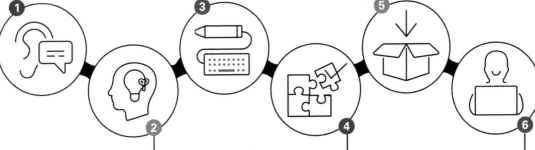

LISTENING & LEARNING

Learn what toys may be popular by:
- asking questions
- listening to children, parents, and companies.

DESIGNING & PROTOTYPING
- Create designs using computers.
- Use designs to create prototype.

SHIPPING & DELIVERING
- Put finished product in boxes.
- Ship to stores and companies.
- Deliver to customers who order online.

BRAINSTORMING & IDEAS
- Use what was learned to come up with ideas for toys.
- Get feedback to decide which toy will be most successful.

MANUFACTURING & CHECKING
- Make each part of toy.
- Combine parts to make finished product.
- Test to make sure finished product is high-quality.

MAKING HAPPY MEMORIES
- Provide support to make sure customers are satisfied.
- Fix or replace products that don't meet quality standards.

H OUTLINE Complete the outline for the description of the process shown in the diagram.

Introduction:

The toy creation process involves six steps.

Step 1: _____

Details: _____

_____

Step 2: _____

Details: _____

_____

Step 3: _____

Details: _____

_____

Step 4: _____

Details: _____

_____

Step 5: _____

Details: _____

_____

Step 6: _____

Details: _____

_____

I FIRST DRAFT Use your outline to write a first draft of your description.

J REVISE Use this list as you write your second draft.

- ☐ Does your description follow a clear organization?
- ☐ Does it summarize all of the necessary information in a clear order?
- ☐ Is there any information that is not needed?

K EDIT Use this list as you write your final draft.

- ☐ Do you use a variety of noun modifiers?
- ☐ Are there any spelling or punctuation errors?

L FINAL DRAFT Reread your description of the process and correct any errors. Then submit it to your teacher.

REFLECT

A Check (✓) the Reflect tasks you can do and the academic skills you can use.

☐ consider the importance of play

☐ make inferences

☐ relate ideas about play to your life

☐ describe a process

☐ consider how design can change behavior

☐ noun modifiers

☐ create a design to change behavior

☐ connect new ideas to what you know

☐ write a description of a diagram

B Write the target words from the unit in the correct column. Add any other words that you learned. Circle words you still need to practice.

NOUN	VERB	ADJECTIVE	ADVERB & OTHER

C Reflect on the ideas in the unit as you answer these questions.

1. Do you agree that play is important for people of all ages? Explain.

_____

_____

2. Albert Einstein once said, "The best design is the simplest one that works." Do you agree or disagree? Why?

_____

_____

3. What is the most important thing you learned in this unit?

_____

_____

OUR ROBOT FUTURE

A robot called TORO with the
director of a robotics group at
the German Aerospace Center
(DLR), Cologne, Germany

IN THIS UNIT

▶ Consider what robots can do

▶ Discuss fictional robots

▶ Predict the abilities of future robots

▶ Support your opinion about AI

▶ Write a summary

SKILLS

READING
Take notes

WRITING
Write a summary

GRAMMAR
Noun clauses

CRITICAL THINKING
Support your opinions

CONNECT TO THE TOPIC

1. Look at the photo. How is the robot like a human? How is it different?

2. Do you have a positive or negative opinion about robots? Explain.

RISE OF THE ROBOBEES

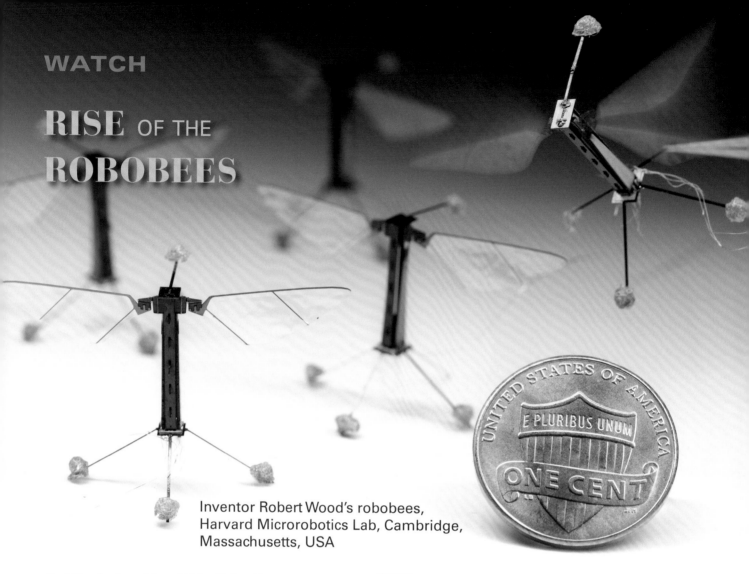

Inventor Robert Wood's robobees, Harvard Microrobotics Lab, Cambridge, Massachusetts, USA

A Watch the video. Write T for *True* or F for *False*. ▶ 4.1

1. _____ Robert Wood studies nature to get ideas for his designs.

2. _____ Wood thinks robobees will mainly be useful in agriculture.

3. _____ When Wood tests the robots, he is usually successful.

4. _____ Wood has developed a robot that is small and can run very fast.

B Watch the video again. Number the ideas (1–5) in the order they are mentioned. ▶ 4.1

a. _____ Robert Wood and his team are building tiny robots to do work that is difficult for humans to do.

b. _____ Robots might help us in homes and hospitals.

c. _____ Science-fiction ideas about helpful robots may soon become true.

d. _____ The team builds and tests, builds and tests.

e. _____ Failure helps Wood's team learn something.

PREPARE TO READ

A VOCABULARY Read the questions. Match the words in bold with their definitions.

1. Do you believe that **artificial** things, such as flowers, can be as beautiful as natural ones?

2. Are you **content** with how much free time you have, or would you like more?

3. What is something you are currently **concerned** about? Why does it worry you?

4. Which relative do you most **resemble**? Your father, mother, or somebody else?

5. Where do you get most of your **knowledge** about the world from? Books, TV, or social media?

6. What food groups do you **lack** in your diet? For example, do you eat enough vegetables?

7. What is a **valid** reason for not doing an assignment? Would your teacher agree that it's a good reason?

8. What is one thing you are **capable of** doing that most people you know cannot do?

9. Have you ever had a project **turn out** better than you hoped? What happened?

10. Can you usually **distinguish** truth from lies?

a. _____ (adj) happy about your situation

b. _____ (adj) made by people; not natural

c. _____ (adj) worried

d. _____ (n) the things you know about a topic

e. _____ (adj phr) able to do something

f. _____ (adj) based on good reasons or facts

g. _____ (v phr) to happen in a particular way

h. _____ (v) to look similar

i. _____ (v) to not have or not have enough

j. _____ (v) to recognize how two things are different

B PERSONALIZE Discuss four or five of the questions from activity A with a partner.

REFLECT Consider what robots can do.

You are going to read about how robots are changing our world. What do you think robots can do in these places today? Discuss your ideas with a small group.

factories   homes   schools   hospitals   stores   offices

An early science-fiction illustration of a robot

ROBOTS:
FROM FICTION TO FACT

A PREVIEW Look at the illustration and read the title. What do they suggest the reading is about? Discuss your ideas with a partner.

1   In 1920, Karel Čapek, a Czech writer, wrote a play called *R.U.R.* In the story, engineers create **artificial** humans that Čapek called robots. These beings look, talk, and think like people. At first, the robots are **content** to work for humans. Soon, they become vital to the world economy. As time passes, humans become **concerned** that robots could be a danger. This worry **turns out** to be **valid**, and eventually the robots take control. Čapek's idea fascinated people everywhere. Since *R.U.R.* was written, there have been thousands of other science-fiction books and movies about robots. But these machines are no longer found only in stories. They exist in real life, and they're changing our world.

2   Some robots **resemble** animals. These robots look or behave like dogs, fish, or birds. They hop like kangaroos, run like dinosaurs, or fly like seagulls. Sometimes engineers design and build these robots to improve their **knowledge** of robots and what they can do. Other animal-like robots, such as robot bees, have been designed to someday perform useful tasks, such as helping farmers grow food. Some companies are creating robots that look and act like pets. These robots could be a good option for people who want a pet but can't keep an animal at home. And because many people feel it's wrong to keep wild animals for entertainment, one company is even developing lifelike[1] robot dolphins that could replace real dolphins in aquariums[2].

3   In addition to animal-like robots, engineers are creating robots that can do dangerous or difficult physical work. These robots can save lives after an earthquake or disaster, explore the deep oceans, or work in outer space. Other robots can do physical tasks that people don't like to do, such as cleaning houses or picking fruit or vegetables. Robots can perform some physical tasks better than people because they work more quickly and make fewer mistakes. Robots can build cars, drive vehicles, build houses, or even prepare pizzas.

4   Bots are different from robots, but they're also changing our world. Bots differ from robots because they exist only inside a computer as a program. In other words, they **lack** a physical body. Early bots had very simple abilities. They could search websites for information but lacked any kind of intelligence. The latest bots are **capable of** truly amazing things. GPT-3, for example, is a bot that can do a wide range of things that only humans could do before. These include translating or summarizing information, writing computer code, and even writing nonfiction articles or creative stories. The writing is so good that some people can't **distinguish** what GPT-3 has written from texts that people have written.

5   In the future, robots and bots will almost certainly become an ever more important part of our world. However, the question that the characters in Čapek's *R.U.R.* asked remains unanswered: Will things be like the start of that story or the end? That is, will robots make our world a better place, or will they be a danger to human society?

---

[1]**lifelike** (adj) just like a living person or thing
[2]**aquarium** (n) a place where people pay to look at fish and other sea animals

READING SKILL   Take notes

Taking notes while you read makes reading a more active process. It can help you better understand an article and remember what you have read. Here is one way to take notes:

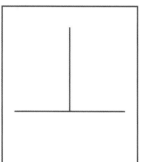

▸ Divide a piece of paper into three sections.
▸ Use the left side to write notes about main ideas.
▸ Use the right side to make notes about key details related to each main idea.
▸ Use the bottom section to write questions you have.

There are many other ways to take notes, such as outlining and mind mapping. Choose a method that is effective for you.

When you take notes, you can save time by not writing full sentences and instead using **symbols** and **abbreviations** such as:

∴ = because	< = less than	→ = relates to
info = information	bec. = because	v. = very
AI = artificial intelligence	KC = Karel Capek	rbt = robot

B APPLY The notes below are for paragraph 1. Write if each note is a *MI* (main idea), *D* (detail), or *Q* (question). Then divide a piece of paper into three sections using the Reading Skill box method. Add the notes to your paper.

1. _____ Karel Čapek → *R.U.R.* about rbts, 1920

2. _____ Rbts common in real life → changing world

3. _____ *R.U.R.* stands for?

4. _____ People concerned rbts will take control

C APPLY Review paragraphs 2–5 and take notes. Compare your notes with a partner.

D MAIN IDEAS Use your notes from activity C to complete the main ideas. Use the phrases from the box. One phrase is extra.

artificial being	excellent design	positive thing
computer program	dangerous work	useful tasks

1. Robots are common in stories because the idea of a(n) _____ is interesting to many people.

2. Some animal-like robots do _____, and others can improve our knowledge.

3. Engineers have created robots that can perform physically _____ that people can't do.

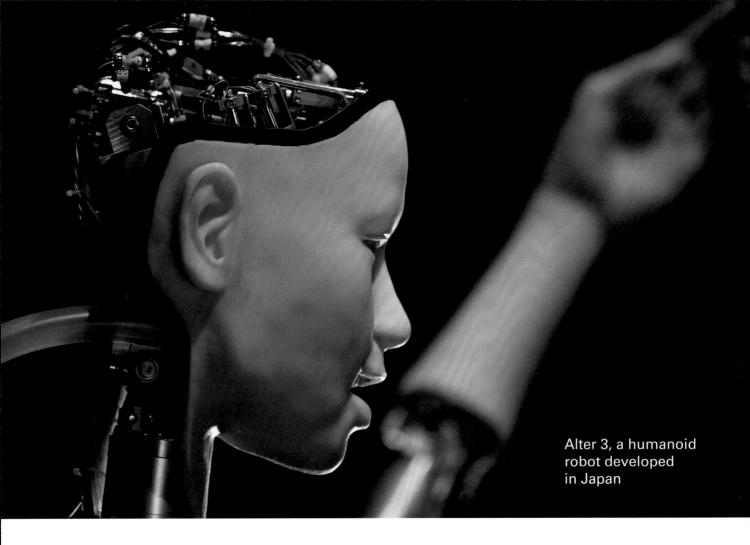

Alter 3, a humanoid robot developed in Japan

4. A bot is a(n) _____ that differs from a robot because it does not have a body.

5. Robots will become more important in the future, but some people are not certain this will be a(n) _____.

E DETAILS Use your notes to answer these questions.

1. About how many years ago did Karel Čapek write *R.U.R.*?

_____

2. What useful thing might robot bees be able to do?

_____

3. In addition to robot bees, what animal-like robots have engineers developed?

_____

4. Why can robots do some things better than people?

_____

5. What kinds of activities can GPT-3 do as well as humans?

_____

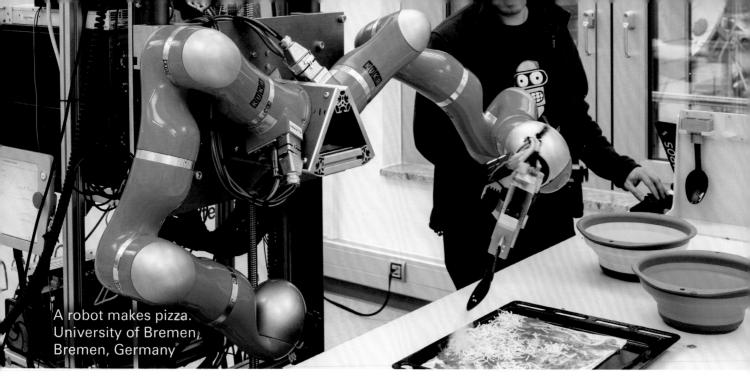

A robot makes pizza.
University of Bremen,
Bremen, Germany

F DETAILS Why does the author . . .

1. begin the article by summarizing Karel Čapek's *R.U.R.*?

    a. To introduce the idea that robots may not always benefit society

    b. To show that sometimes things that people predict come true

2. refer to dinosaurs, seagulls, and kangaroos in paragraph 2?

    a. To give examples of robots that were built to improve engineers' knowledge

    b. To compare the abilities of animal robots with robots that resemble humans

3. mention that robots can do dangerous or difficult work in paragraph 3?

    a. To suggest that robots are only useful in a few situations

    b. To point out that robots can do things that benefit society

4. include so many things that the GPT-3 bot can do?

    a. To explain how this bot was developed

    b. To show how advanced this bot is

5. end the article by asking a question about the future?

    a. To suggest that some predictions can never be proved

    b. To repeat a key idea introduced earlier in the article

REFLECT   Discuss fictional robots.

Think about a story from a book, movie, game, or TV show that has a robot in it. Answer the questions in your notebook. Then tell a partner about your story.

1. What is the story mainly about?

2. What does the robot look like? What can the robot do?

3. How do the people in the story react to the robot? Why?

PREPARE TO READ

A VOCABULARY Read the definitions. Then complete each sentence with the correct form of the words.

complex (adj) difficult to understand
consequence (n) the result of something
direct (v) to guide actions
inevitable (adj) certain to happen
optimistic (adj) positive about the future
prospect (n) something that may happen
resource (n) money, materials, or other things that can be used to reach a goal
responsibility (n) something you have to do; a duty
vast (adj) huge; enormous
wisdom (n) knowledge, experience, good judgment

1. I don't like to _____ other people. In fact, I prefer others telling *me* what to do.

2. I was kind of negative when I was younger, but I'm more _____ now.

3. I like playing video games, but in general I prefer simple games to _____ ones.

4. I think it's _____ that robots will change our world a lot.

5. I've made some mistakes in my life, but luckily none have had serious _____.

6. In general, I think that older people have more _____ than younger people.

7. One of the most important _____ at a school or university is the library.

8. There's a _____ difference between phones now and phones from 20 years ago.

9. When I am given a task to do, I feel that it's my _____ to do it as well as possible.

10. The _____ of robots taking over the world doesn't seem very likely.

B PERSONALIZE Which statements from activity A do you agree with? Discuss with a partner.

REFLECT Predict the abilities of future robots.

You are going to read two opinion articles about the future of robots. Check the statements that you agree with. Add your own ideas. Then discuss your opinions with a small group.

In the future, robots and bots will . . .

☐ paint pictures that are as good as ones by human artists.
☐ do most jobs that humans do now.
☐ sound like a real person.
☐ write books that are as good as ones written by human authors.
☐ Other: _____
☐ Other: _____

READ

A PREVIEW Skim the two articles and choose the best description.

a. One writer expresses positive views, and the other one expresses negative views.

b. One writer expresses both positive and negative views; the other is just positive.

c. One writer gives only negative opinions; the other is both positive and negative.

A ROBOT FUTURE? NOT SO FAST!

🎧 4.2

1   Like many people, I think humanlike robots and artificial intelligence (AI) are just around the corner[1]. Fei-Fei Li, a computer scientist at Stanford University, suggests that "AI is going to make us work more productively[2], live longer, and have cleaner energy." I hope she's right, but I'm less **optimistic** than she is.

Robots working at the check-in counter, Henn na Hotel ("Strange Hotel"), Nagasaki, Japan

2 On one hand, artificial intelligence is already benefiting society. In late 2020, an AI developed by a company named DeepMind found an answer to a problem that humans were unable to solve for 50 years. The AI was able to suggest how unfamiliar proteins[3] might affect the body by predicting the shape they would have. This knowledge will help scientists better understand new diseases, which often contain unknown proteins, and develop medicines more effectively and cheaply.

3 On the other hand, the **prospect** that robots or AI might cause problems for society has been described in stories for many years. And in recent years, it has gone from being fiction to fact. Many people have lost their jobs to robots and computers. And a recent report suggests that up to 800 million more people—that's roughly the population of the United States, Brazil, Mexico, and Japan combined—might lose their jobs in the next 10 years.

4 The opposite situation happened in 2019. At the time, a Japanese company owned a hotel that was run by robots. Unfortunately, they kept making mistakes, such as waking guests up at night. The company eventually had to "fire" the robots and hire humans to replace many of them. Robots and AI shouldn't make mistakes, but they're designed and trained by humans, who *do* make errors. Waking people up is a minor problem, but I think it's **inevitable** that at some point, a robot or AI will make a major error. And that could have serious **consequences**.

5 The famous science-fiction author Isaac Asimov said that "Science gathers knowledge faster than society gathers **wisdom**." I think Asimov is right. Before we give control to AI, shouldn't we first develop the wisdom to control our own intelligence?

---

[1]**just around the corner** (phr) coming very soon

[2]**productively** (adv) producing or achieving a lot

[3]**protein** (n) a natural substance that is necessary for growth and strength

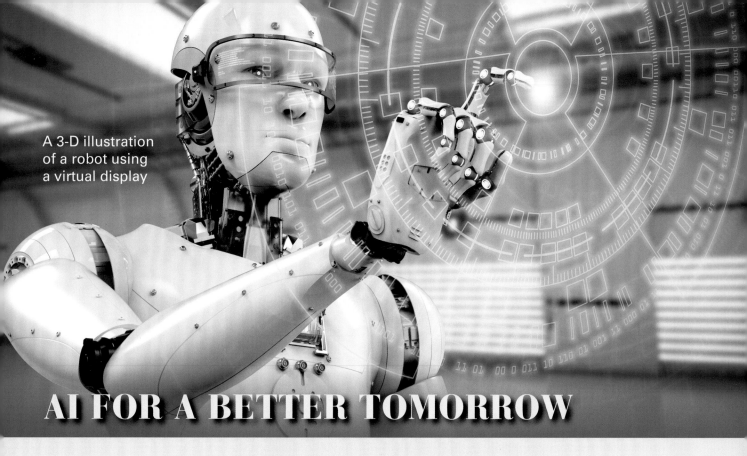

A 3-D illustration of a robot using a virtual display

AI FOR A BETTER TOMORROW

1   Almost every culture has myths[1] about machines eventually becoming more powerful than their creators and then trying to kill them. Nobody really knows what the future holds, and it's human nature to be afraid of the unknown. However, machines were created by people, so it's only logical that they should help people.

2   People are interested in AI because of the potential dangers, but I don't think artificial intelligence is something to fear. I believe it is a very powerful tool that can improve the planet for humans. With the right **resources**, AI can benefit humanity because it will allow us to do things much more efficiently and expand our knowledge and understanding.

3   Machines are able to do many things that humans cannot do. Computers can calculate things much faster than any human. They can remember **vast** amounts of information, and they never forget. They can control larger and more **complex** machines than any one human could ever control. In other words, computers do a better job at many things.

4   But it's not the computer that does the work; it's just a tool. It's like asking, "Why is a calculator better at math than humans?" It's a tool designed to do a specific set of operations. In this case, a computer is designed to use algorithms[2] to solve problems. Human minds are not as good at this sort of thing, as is shown by the need for inventing the calculator in the first place.

5   I believe technology can be scary, but it's what we make of it. It can do a lot of good if we use it right and if we make an effort to control it. We built it, so it's our **responsibility** to at least help **direct** it in some way. However, I also believe we should let AI do some things on its own and that we *do* have the wisdom to control machine intelligence.

---

[1]**myth** (n) an untrue story or idea that many people believe
[2]**algorithms** (n) programming instructions that help computers solve problems

B MAIN IDEAS Read the statements. Where is each idea stated? Write R (*A Robot Future? Not So Fast!*), AI (*AI for a Better Tomorrow*), B (both texts), or N (neither text).

1. _____ Computers and artificial intelligence are powerful tools that people can control.

2. _____ Most people don't mind robots that look human but are less sure about other intelligent machines.

3. _____ Artificial intelligence can do things people cannot do and can improve our lives.

4. _____ Robots and AI have already had a negative effect on society, and this may get worse.

C MAIN IDEAS One of the articles was written by a human, and the other by a bot. Which article do you think was written by a bot and why? Discuss your ideas with a partner.

D DETAILS Complete each statement with one of the phrases (a–f).

a. kinds of tools   d. resources and support

b. a lot of information   e. robots or computers

c. hotel in Japan   f. science-fiction writer

1. A famous _____ thinks society needs to develop greater wisdom.

2. A large number of people have already lost their jobs to _____.

3. AI was able to find _____ about proteins.

4. Computers and other machines are _____ that can help people.

5. With enough _____, AI can make the world a better place.

6. Its robot staff made many mistakes, so a _____ had to hire humans.

CRITICAL THINKING   **Support your opinions**

After you have read an article, you may be asked to express an opinion about it. To do this, think carefully about how the information in the article can support your opinion. For example, if you want to explain why you think a writer's point of view is too optimistic, review the reading and your notes to find information that shows the negative side of the topic.

REFLECT   Support your opinion about AI.

Answer the questions. Then share your opinions in a small group.

1. Do you think that robots and AI will help or harm us? Support your opinion with information from the articles and your own ideas.

2. Which article do you think has the more convincing arguments? Explain.

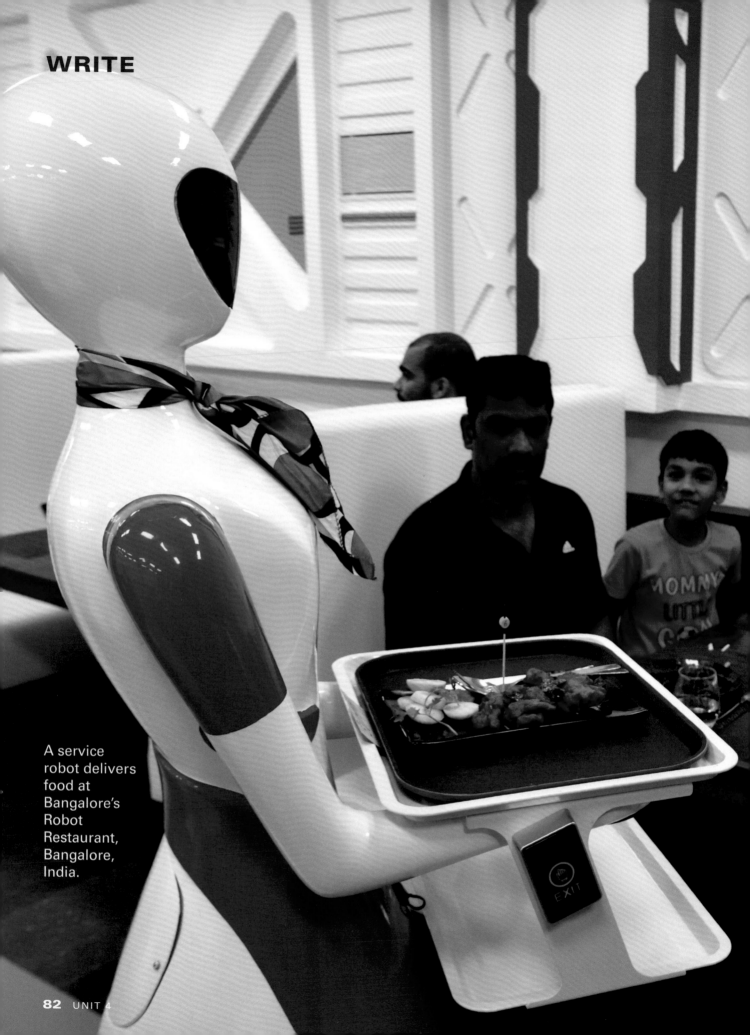

WRITE

A service robot delivers food at Bangalore's Robot Restaurant, Bangalore, India.

EXIT

Write a summary.

You are going to write a one-paragraph summary of a text about robots. Use the ideas, vocabulary, and skills from the unit.

A MODEL Read the two model summaries of the article *Robots: From Fiction to Fact*. Make some notes about which summary you think is better, and why.

Summary 1

In the article *Robots: From Fiction to Fact,* the writer describes different types of new robots and discusses how they might change the world. The writer first explains that robots began as an idea in a play by Karel Čapek. The writer then describes real robots that look and act like animals including bees and dolphins. He says that these animal-like robots help engineers design more useful robots. The writer next introduces the idea that robots can do work instead of people. For example, robots can clean homes, make food, and drive cars. The writer then describes computer programs called bots. He mentions that early bots were not very advanced. In contrast, modern bots can write almost as well as people. The writer concludes by arguing that bots and robots will become even more important in the future and by questioning whether this will be good or bad for society.

Summary 2

The article *Robots: From Fiction to Fact* includes a lot of really interesting information about robots in stories and real life. The writer's main idea is that robots might take control of it. This worries me a lot! The first robots appeared in a play called *R.U.R.* by Karel Čapek. The robots in Čapek's play sound like they were really dangerous to people. According to the author, engineers have also designed robots that are like animals. These include robot dinosaurs that run, seagulls that fly, bees that help farmers, pets that are good for people who don't want a real animal, and even dolphins that could replace real ones in aquariums. Other robots can do physical work that is dangerous or difficult, such as pick fruit or vegetables or prepare pizzas. Bots are like robots but also different from them. Some are advanced, and some are simple. One example is GPT-3, which has very advanced computer code that was written by people. In conclusion, I think the writer's arguments are interesting, but I am not sure I agree with the writer's suggestion that robots and bots will pose a danger to human society.

WRITING SKILL Write a summary

When you summarize a text, you restate the main points and important details of the original. A summary should be shorter than the original—about one-third as long or less—and should include different words from the original when possible. A summary does not add to or change the original text's ideas. You also do not express your opinion in a summary.

You can organize your summary in the following way:

▶ Begin with an introductory sentence that gives the author's name (if known) and the title of the text.
▶ Add a thesis statement that gives the overall main idea of the text. You can also mention the author's purpose if you know or can infer it.
▶ Add a new sentence for each main point in the text. Include the main supporting details, either in the same sentence or in a new sentence.
▶ Finish with a concluding sentence that restates the thesis and overall main point.

B ANALYZE THE MODEL Compare the two summaries with the original article. Check (✓) the correct column in the chart.

	Summary 1	Summary 2
1. It is shorter than the article.		
2. It mainly uses different words.		
3. It includes all the main points.		
4. It gives important supporting details for each main point.		
5. It avoids adding personal opinions or other ideas.		

C ANALYZE THE MODEL Complete the tasks.

1. Which do you think is the better summary? Summary 1 or Summary 2? _____
2. Highlight the thesis statement in that summary.
3. Highlight the concluding sentence.
4. Explain why you think the summary you chose is better.

_____

_____

GRAMMAR Noun clauses

A noun clause functions as a noun in a sentence. Noun clauses always include a subject and a verb, but do not stand alone.

A noun clause can be the subject of a sentence:
> **Why it happened** *is not clear to me.*

A noun clause can be the object of a verb, infinitive, or gerund:
> *He said* **that we should consider it**.
> *It's not easy to explain* **how AI works**.
> *Believing* **that AI can solve all our problems** *is a mistake.*

A noun clause can come after *be* or another linking verb:
> *This is* **what we need to do.**

Noun clauses usually begin with a subordinator. The subordinator *that* is used after reporting verbs such as *discuss*, *explain*, *mention*, or *say* and thinking verbs such as *believe*, *feel*, or *think*.

Other subordinators are the *wh-* question words *how*, *what*, *where*, *when*, *which*, *who*, and *why*. We use statement word order and no question mark with noun clauses that start with *wh-* words.
> ✗ The robot doesn't care ~~where does it work~~?
> ✓ The robot doesn't care **where it works**.

Note: You can omit *that* in noun clauses: *He said ~~that~~ we should consider it.*

D GRAMMAR Find and underline these noun clauses in the first model summary.
A noun clause that is . . .

1. the object of *discuss.*
2. the object of *explain.*
3. the object of *mention.*
4. the object of a gerund.
5. the object of *question.*

E GRAMMAR Complete the sentences with words from the box.

how	that	what	when	where	whether	why

1. It's hard to explain _____ some people worry about robots.

2. Many people are interested in knowing _____ robots are made.

3. Some experts say _____ humanlike robots will soon exist.

4. The year 1920 is _____ the word *robot* was first used.

5. We don't know _____ machines will be a danger to society.

6. _____ some artificial intelligence can do is really amazing.

F GRAMMAR Complete this conversation with noun clauses from the box.

that it could be joking	what I must do	where I can hide
that it might be dangerous	what's wrong	why you would say that

A: You look worried. Do you want to tell me ¹_____?

B: It's my new robot. I think ²_____. It keeps saying, "Taking control of the world is ³_____!"

A: Hmm. It doesn't *look* dangerous. Do you think ⁴_____?

B: Joking?! I don't know ⁵_____. It's a HAL-9000 robot: They don't joke.

A: That's true. I don't think you need to be concerned, though. It's probably nothing.

B: You're right. But I'm going to decide ⁶_____ if it does attack.

G GRAMMAR Read the quotations. Then answer the questions with noun clauses.

"People are fascinated with robots because they are reflections of ourselves."—Ken Goldberg, professor at University of California, Berkeley

"I think people will have . . . friendships with robots in the future."—Cynthia Breazeal, professor at Massachusetts Institute of Technology

1. What does Ken Goldberg believe about people?

   _____

2. What does Cynthia Breazeal suggest about the future?

   _____

LEARNING TIP

Don't confuse noun clauses with adjective clauses. Noun clauses with *that* usually come after a verb (*I know that I'm late.*). Adjective clauses with *that* usually come after a noun. (*The robot that I want is expensive.*)

A robotic dog on display, Lisbon, Portugal

H EDIT Find and correct five errors with noun clauses in this summary of a video.

The video *Rise of the Robobees* describes how are Robert Wood and his team are developing robots based on animals. They are currently working on robobees. Wood says what these tiny robots could be useful in many ways, such as exploring dangerous places or helping with agriculture. The team tests their robots many times, and Wood explains who these tests often go wrong. However, every failure helps them move closer to success. Wood and his team have also developed a robot that can run faster than Usain Bolt. Wood describes how can this robot climb on different kinds of material. At the end of the video, Wood talks about creating robots that can interact gently with people. Wood is excited because he believes when robots will affect people's lives in positive ways soon.

PLAN & WRITE

I OUTLINE Complete these steps.

1. Read the opinion article *A Robot Future? Not So Fast!* again and take notes.
2. Review your notes; delete any minor details or personal opinions.
3. Use information from your notes to complete this outline of a summary of the text.

Article title: _____

Author's purpose: _____

Thesis statement: _____

First main point: _____

    Supporting info: _____

Second main point: _____

    Supporting info: _____

Third main point: _____

    Supporting info: _____

Conclusion: _____

WRITING TIP

When writing a summary, it is important to paraphrase the original text. Paraphrasing means writing the ideas of a text in your own words. To change an original text into your own words, do some or all of the following:

1. Underline or highlight key words in the original text.
2. Replace these key words with synonyms or short phrases that have the same meaning.
3. Change parts of speech (e.g., verbs into the noun form, nouns into adjectives).
4. Use different sentence structures.

J FIRST DRAFT Use your outline to write a first draft of your summary.

K REVISE Use this list as you write your second draft.

☐ Is your summary shorter than the original article?

☐ Does it have an introductory sentence that mentions the title of the article?

☐ Does it include a thesis statement that states the main idea of the article?

☐ Does your summary restate all of the main points in a logical order?

☐ Is each main point supported with key details?

☐ Does your summary have a concluding sentence that restates the main point?

L EDIT Use this list as you write your final draft.

☐ Does your summary use noun clauses?

☐ Can synonyms replace any words repeated from the original?

M FINAL DRAFT Reread your final draft and correct any errors. Then submit it to your teacher.

Robby the Robot in a scene from the 1956 science-fiction film *Forbidden Planet*

REFLECT

A Check (✓) the Reflect activities you can do and the academic skills you can use.

☐ Consider what robots can do

☐ Discuss fictional robots

☐ Predict the abilities of future robots

☐ Support your opinion about artificial intelligence

☐ Write a summary

☐ Take notes

☐ Write a summary

☐ Noun clauses

☐ Support your opinions

B Write the vcoabulary words from the unit in the correct column. Add any other words that you learned. Circle words you still need to practice.

NOUN	VERB	ADJECTIVE	ADVERB & OTHER

C Reflect on the ideas in the unit as you answer these questions.

1. In general, how do you feel about robots and intelligent machines: concerned, excited, or something else? Why?

   _____

   _____

2. Do you think humans and robots will ever develop friendships?

   _____

   _____

3. What is the most important thing you learned in this unit?

   _____

   _____

THERE IS NO PLANET B

▶ Consider the impact of inventions

▶ Discuss the pros and cons of "green" actions

▶ Consider what makes a solution innovative

▶ Evaluate innovations

▶ Write a problem-solution essay about an environmental issue

SKILLS

READING
Understand references within a text

WRITING
Organize a problem-solution essay

GRAMMAR
Pronouns and related words

CRITICAL THINKING
Evaluate solutions

An oil pipeline

CONNECT TO THE TOPIC

1. What problem or problems does this photograph illustrate?

2. What do you think "There is no Planet B" means? In what ways do you think Earth needs our help?

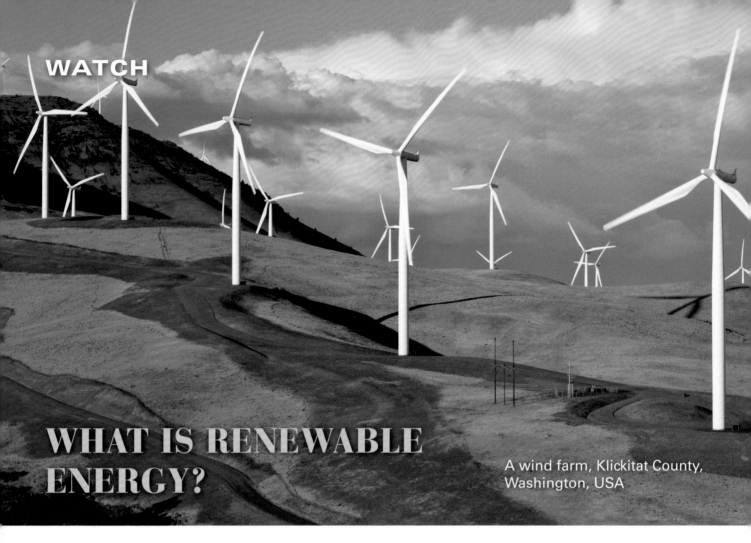

WHAT IS RENEWABLE ENERGY?

A wind farm, Klickitat County, Washington, USA

A Watch the first part of the video. Choose the correct word or phrase to complete each statement. ▶ 5.1

1. Renewable energy comes from sources that replenish themselves and **do not** / **rarely** run out.

2. Some common kinds of renewable energy include solar, **weather** / **wind**, hydro, geothermal, and biomass.

3. More than **18** / **80** percent of the energy that people currently use comes from fossil fuels.

4. Currently, renewables are the **fastest** / **slowest** growing source of energy in the world.

B Watch the whole video. Choose the statement that best summarizes the main idea of the video. ▶ 5.2

a. Although renewable energy costs more than energy from fossil fuels, it's a better energy source because it has no disadvantages.

b. Although renewable energy has some disadvantages, its advantages mean that it is a good alternative to fossil fuels.

c. Although most people now prefer energy from renewable sources, fossil fuels may become popular again in the future.

C Work in small groups. Discuss the questions.

1. Are any kinds of renewable energy common or important in your country?

2. Would you be happy to pay more for energy from renewable sources? Why or why not?

PREPARE TO READ

A VOCABULARY Match the bold words and their roots (word parts to which we add prefixes and suffixes) to the correct definition.

1. _____ **decade** (*dec* = ten)
2. _____ **equivalent** (*equi* = the same or equal)
3. _____ **generate** (*gen* = produce or give birth)
4. _____ **innovation** (*nov* = new)
5. _____ **progress** (*pro* = forward; *gress* = walk)

a. a new idea or invention
b. a period of 10 years
c. to produce
d. movement toward a better situation
e. equal to something else

B VOCABULARY Read the sentences. Write the correct form of the bold words next to their definitions.

▶ Smartphones have many **features** that make them useful and easy to use.

▶ Some cities **have banned** plastic shopping bags as a way of protecting the environment.

▶ Many significant technological **advances**, such as the microchip, occurred in the 20th century.

▶ A **principle** that many inventors **take into account** today is that inventions should help to protect the environment.

1. _____ (n) an improvement

2. _____ (n) a rule for doing something in the right way

3. _____ (n) a distinctive aspect

4. _____ (v phr) to consider when making a decision

5. _____ (v) to not allow; to prohibit

C PERSONALIZE Discuss these questions with a partner.

1. Which **features** of your phone are the most useful to you?
2. Do you agree that **banning** plastic shopping bags can help protect the environment? Explain.
3. What should you **take into account** before you choose a career?

REFLECT Consider the impact of inventions.

You're going to read about the impact of an invention. Write some notes about the impacts—both good and bad—of the products below. Then share your ideas with a partner.

▶ electric cars   ▶ refrigerators   ▶ fitness trackers   ▶ smartphones

COOL INVENTION?

A PREDICT The passage is about the invention of the air conditioner. Choose two meanings of "cool" that you think are implied by the title. Then scan the text to confirm your ideas.

a. calm

b. fashionable

c. neither too hot nor cold

d. not friendly

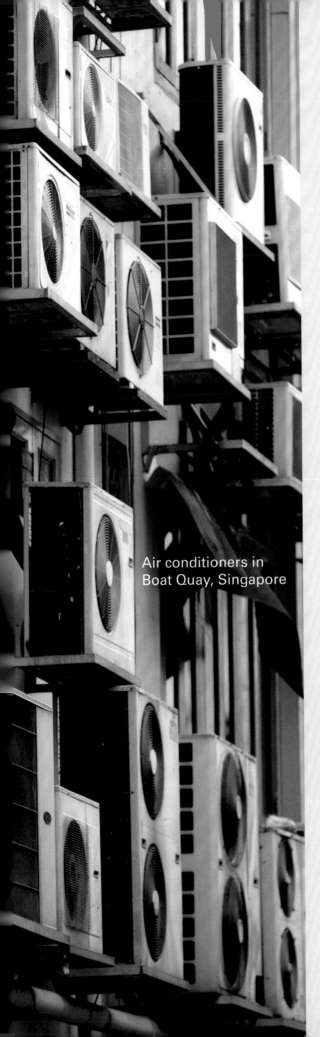

Air conditioners in Boat Quay, Singapore

 5.1

1   One striking **feature** of the 20th and 21st centuries is the speed of technological **progress**. Put simply, there are more new inventions now than at any time in human history. As a general rule, technology improves our lives in some way. Many inventions are designed to make it easier for us to deal with our environment. They may, for example, help keep us warm or stay safe. As the Canadian philosopher Marshall McLuhan said, "Technology is that which separates us from our environment." But, while inventions *do* help us enjoy the environment in which we live and protect us from it, <u>they</u> don't always make the world a better place.

2   Many technological **advances** *have* made our lives easier. Modern vehicles allow us to travel long distances quickly and easily. The Internet makes it easy to buy different products whenever we want. However, some developments have actually added to the environmental problems the world faces today. We know that cars and other vehicles add to air pollution. This increased level of pollution not only causes the planet to become warmer but can also make us sick. And plastic of all sorts has found <u>its</u> way into every part of our environment. Experts believe that eight million tons of plastic enter the oceans every year. <u>That's</u> **equivalent** to more than 500,000 full garbage trucks.

3   Another example of an advance that both solves and causes problems is arguably one of the most important **innovations** of the early 20th century: the air conditioner. The air conditioner was invented in 1902 by an American engineer named Willis Carrier. Air conditioners were not widespread in the United States until the late 1940s. In the **decades** since, their popularity has grown tremendously. Today, nearly 90 percent of U.S. homes have air conditioners. They are also found all over the world. The reason for this massive growth in popularity is obvious: air conditioners make life much more comfortable. <u>This</u> is especially true in places such as Jakarta, Hong Kong, and Riyadh, which have, in that order, tropical[1], subtropical[2], and desert climates.

4   The reasons air conditioners have a negative impact on the environment are not obvious, but they are simple to explain. First, air conditioners need a *lot* of power to run. <u>This</u> is a problem because **generating** the necessary power contributes to[3] climate change. In the past, countries such as South Korea and Bangladesh actually **banned** air conditioners because of

---

[1]**tropical** (adj) extremely hot and humid

[2]**subtropical** (adj) usually hot and humid

[3]**contribute to** (v phr) to help cause

how much power they use. The second problem is that air conditioners use a special gas, commonly known as freon, to cool air. If freon gets into the atmosphere—for example when an air conditioner breaks down or is thrown away—<u>it</u> traps[4] heat from the sun. This also contributes to climate change. In other words, when we use air conditioners to cool our buildings down, we're actually heating our planet up.

5   Why have important and useful inventions like the air conditioner also had a negative effect on our world? It's *not* a lack of ingenuity[5]. The last 125 years have proven that humans are able to create incredible innovations to improve our lives. Rather, the problem is that the focus of inventors is often on immediate solutions, not on solutions that **take the future into account**. An alternative approach is to use the "seventh-generation **principle**"—an idea that comes from the Haudenosaunee, an American Indian group of nations. This principle suggests that whenever we take actions or make decisions, we should consider seven generations into the future (about 140 years). In other words, the environment is not just ours. We are keeping <u>it</u> safe for our children and their children.

[4]**trap** (v) to keep in a place
[5]**ingenuity** (n) the ability to think of clever ways to do something

Delivering ice
for cooling, 1918

B MAIN IDEAS Complete the main ideas by matching the beginning of each statement to its ending.

1. There have been many advances that have made life easier, _____.

2. Air conditioners became a popular and important innovation _____.

3. One problem with air conditioners is that they keep buildings cool, _____.

4. Inventors can come up with innovations that protect the planet _____.

a. because they make people's lives more comfortable.

b. but some have affected the environment negatively.

c. but they also cause Earth's climate to become hotter.

d. if they take both the present and future into account.

C DETAILS Read each statement. Write T for *True*, F for *False*, or NG for *Not Given*.

1. _____ Technological progress is faster now than it was at earlier times in history.

2. _____ Garbage trucks generally carry more plastic than other kinds of trash.

3. _____ Willis Carrier invented the air conditioner to help keep his home cool.

4. _____ Air conditioners became popular almost immediately in the United States.

5. _____ Jakarta, Hong Kong, and Riyadh all have different climates.

6. _____ People in Bangladesh are not currently allowed to use air conditioners.

7. _____ The production of freon gas is a significant cause of climate change.

> **LEARNING TIP**
>
> Reading can help you become a better writer. As you read, look for how the writer
> ▶ creates interest in a topic.
> ▶ uses synonyms instead of repeating words.

D Answer these questions about paragraph 2. Then share your ideas with a partner.

1. What examples of efficiency does the writer give? _____

2. What word introduces a contrasting idea? _____

3. What noun is a synonym of *advances*? _____

4. Why does the writer mention 500,000 full garbage trucks? _____

_____

READING SKILL   Understand references within a text

To avoid repetition, writers often use pronouns and other words to refer to information mentioned in other places in a text. To understand the passage, you need to understand what these pronouns and other words refer to. For example:

Air conditioners were not widespread until *the late 1940s*. Since **then**, **their** popularity has grown.

You may also see references to longer ideas with *this/that/these/those* (+ noun phrase). For example:

Air conditioners are also found all over the world. The reason for **this** is obvious.

Air conditioners are also found all over the world. The reason for **this massive growth in popularity** is obvious.

Note: *this* + noun phrase makes the reference clearer.

E APPLY Read the excerpt. Choose the word or phrase that **some** refers to.

Many technological advances have made our lives easier. Modern vehicles allow people to travel long distances quickly and easily. The Internet makes it easy to buy different products whenever we want. However, **some** have actually added to the environmental problems the world faces today.

a. technological advances   b. vehicles   c. people   d. different products

F APPLY Find the underlined word in the article and write the word or words it refers to.

1. they (para. 1) _____

2. its (para. 2) _____

3. That's (para. 2) _____

4. This (para. 3) _____

5. This (para. 4) _____

6. it (para. 4) _____

7. it (para. 5) _____

REFLECT   Discuss the pros and cons of "green" actions.

The article suggests that we "consider seven generations into the future" when we take actions or make decisions." Using this principle, discuss the pros and cons of the actions below.

1. A farmer plants hundreds of trees in a large field.

2. A city bans cars from the streets on weekends.

3. A business stops using plastic in all its products.

4. A commuter cycles to work.

PREPARE TO READ

A VOCABULARY Discuss the meanings of the bold words with a partner. Then match the words to their definitions.

1. Batteries **store** power when they are charged and **release** it when they're used.
2. Air conditioners release **excess** heat outside. This raises outdoor temperatures.
3. Companies that **currently** cause a lot of pollution sometimes claim they will pollute less in the future. However, there's no **guarantee** that they will do this.
4. People usually worry during a **crisis**, but bad situations can also lead to opportunities.
5. Weather forecasts can be **unreliable**; it might rain when the forecast says it will be fine.
6. The bicycle is an **efficient** vehicle; most of a rider's energy is used to move it forward.
7. When inventors take the right **approach**, advances in technology can help us **conquer** some of the problems that the world faces.

1. _____ (adj) not always accurate or correct

2. _____ (adj) extra or too much

3. _____ (adj) wasting little time, energy, or money

4. _____ (adv) at the present; right now

5. _____ (n) a difficult or dangerous situation

6. _____ (n) a promise that something will happen or be done

7. _____ (n) a way to think about or do something

8. _____ (v) to let go of

9. _____ (v) to deal with or fight against a problem successfully

10. _____ (v) to keep something so it can be used later

B PERSONALIZE Discuss these questions in a small group.

1. What kinds of information do you **store** on your phone and computer?
2. What's the most **efficient approach** for you to learn new words?

REFLECT   Consider what makes a solution innovative.

You're going to read about innovative solutions to environmental problems. Read the factors that are important to consider and add your own ideas. Check the two that you think are the most important. Then discuss your ideas with a partner.

An innovative solution to an environmental problem . . .

☐ is cheaper than traditional approaches.   ☐ uses natural materials.
☐ uses new technology.   ☐ _____
☐ makes a lot of money.   ☐ _____

READ

INNOVATIVE IDEAS FOR
THE ENVIRONMENT

A PREVIEW Skim the article. What does the text discuss: problems, solutions, or both?

🎧 5.2

1   Technology has added to many of the environmental problems that are **currently** affecting us. Despite this, thoughtful innovations may solve some of them. Ecologist Barry Commoner wrote that "The proper use of science is not to **conquer** nature but to live in it." In other words, in order to make our world a safe home for future generations, inventors and scientists need to take the environment into account when developing new technology.

2   Most of the world's power is still generated by burning fossil fuels. This has a huge effect on the environment, so for decades scientists have been developing ways to generate power from renewable sources such as the sun, wind, and waves. However, renewable energy production can be **unreliable** because it depends on nature. On some days, there may be too little power; on other days, there may be too much, and the energy may get wasted because it's hard to **store**. One group of scientists might have an innovative solution. They have found a way to store power in bricks[1] cheaply and safely. If houses of the future were made from these bricks, millions of homes could store and **release** power as needed. This could make renewable energy a far more reliable power source.

3   Cooling and heating homes and offices is a major cause of environmental problems because both require so much power. Some scientists have

---

[1] **brick** (n) a clay block used for making houses and other buildings

A "bubble barrier" at work in a canal in Amsterdam, the Netherlands

invented a special fabric[2] to make clothes that can move heat away from the skin to keep people cool. This is an especially innovative solution because cooling one individual is much more **efficient** than doing the same for a whole building. Others have thought outside the box[3] and come up with creative ideas for heating. The subway trains that run under cities like London produce plenty of unwanted heat. Factories often produce **excess** heat, too. Many different groups are working on ways to take this heat and use it to keep businesses, schools, and homes warm.

4   Unfortunately, even with innovative ways to store renewable energy and make cooling and heating more environmentally friendly, climate change will continue. This is because of the amount of carbon dioxide (CO_2) in the atmosphere. CO_2 makes our planet warmer by trapping the sun's heat. Because plants remove CO_2 from the air, planting more trees could help, and this is happening on a global scale right now. In Africa, for example, 21 nations—from Senegal in the west to Djibouti in the east—are working together to plant a Great Green Wall of trees 4,650 miles (7,600 kilometers) across the continent. But planting trees is expensive, so scientists are working on other solutions. One idea is to create artificial leaves. These will not only remove more CO_2 from the air than regular leaves but also turn the CO_2 into a useful fuel.

[2]**fabric** (n) a material used for making clothes

[3]**think outside the box** (v phr) think in an original or creative way

5   Like CO_2, plastic needs to be removed from the environment. One clever **approach** involves using a machine that creates bubbles at the bottom of a river. As they rise, the bubbles push waste plastic to one side of the river where it can easily be collected. Tests show that the bubbles work effectively and are no danger to fish or other creatures in the water. In theory, the same technology could also be used to clean up our oceans. Scientists are also developing ways to deal with plastic after it has been collected. One group found bacteria that can eat plastic and get energy from it. The scientists hope that within a few years, these bacteria will make it possible to recycle plastic completely.

6   Will these thoughtful, inventive ideas help us? There is no **guarantee** that they will all be effective solutions, but some of them will surely work. And hundreds of thousands of smart people are working on other ideas, too, so there's every reason to hope that the current climate **crisis** may soon become a climate celebration.

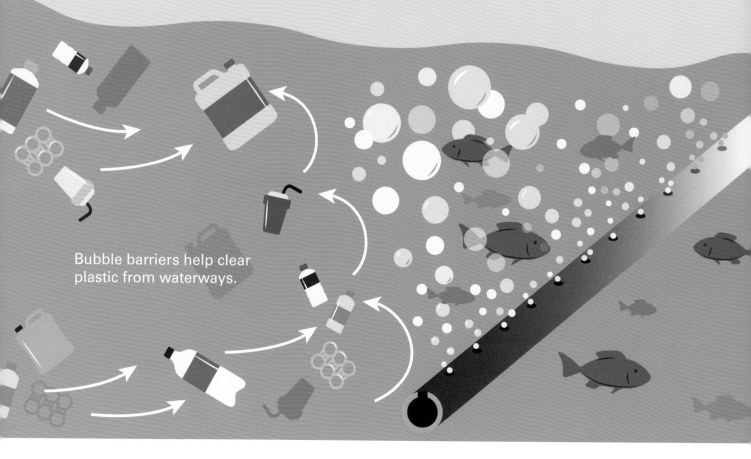

Bubble barriers help clear plastic from waterways.

B MAIN IDEAS Complete each main idea with a phrase from the box. One phrase is extra.

clever scientists	efficient approaches	renewable energy
climate change	environmental issues	two steps

1.   Technology might solve some of the _____ that it has caused.

2.   _____ is good, but it can sometimes be unreliable.

3.   Several _____ to cooling and heating are under development.

4.   Removing CO_2 from the atmosphere can help reduce or limit _____.

5.   There are _____ to dealing with plastic waste: collect it and break it down.

C DETAILS Complete the descriptions of the solutions for each problem. Use one word from the article for each answer.

1. When there's too much renewable _____, some power is wasted. One solution is to store the power in _____ and then release it when it is needed.

2. Carbon dioxide (CO_2) can trap the sun's heat. Artificial leaves can produce _____ from CO_2 that they remove from the _____.

3. Rivers are increasingly polluted by plastic. A _____ releases bubbles that rise and push _____ to the side of a river without hurting _____.

CRITICAL THINKING   Evaluate solutions

When you read about a solution to a problem, evaluate whether it is a reasonable idea. Think about the pros (the good points or strengths) and the cons (the bad points or weaknesses) of the idea. If the pros are stronger than the cons, it's probably a good solution.

D APPLY Match the solutions described in the article, a–c, to the possible pros and cons. Then check (✓) the pros and cons that are mentioned in the article.

Solution	Possible Pros	Possible Cons
1. _____	▶ Makes a source of power more reliable ▶ Can be used to construct places to live	▶ May be unattractive or unfashionable ▶ May be expensive to do or make
2. _____	▶ Helps people feel more comfortable ▶ Produces something people use every day	▶ May not be useful at all times of year ▶ May be unattractive or unfashionable
3. _____	▶ Makes use of something unwanted ▶ Available in many cities and large towns	▶ May not be useful at all times of year ▶ May be expensive to do or make

a. Keeping people cool with special clothes

b. Storing renewable energy in bricks

c. Using excess heat to warm buildings

REFLECT   Evaluate innovations.

In a small group, brainstorm the pros and cons of the solutions. Decide which solution you think would have the most impact on the environment.

1. Removing CO_2 with a wall of trees in Africa

2. Removing CO_2 with artificial leaves

3. Collecting plastic waste with a bubble barrier

4. Breaking down plastic waste using bacteria

Fish sculpture made of recycled plastic, Helsingør, Denmark

UNIT TASK   Write a problem-solution essay about an environmental issue.

You are going to write an essay that describes an environmental problem and proposes solutions. Use the ideas, vocabulary, and skills from the unit.

A MODEL Read the essay. Highlight the specific problems related to plastic waste mentioned in the first paragraph.

Solutions to the Problem of Plastic Waste

Plastic waste has become a major environmental problem. One estimate says that around eight million tons of plastic enter the oceans every year. This is a problem because plastic waste looks unattractive. In addition, small bits of plastic can get into the bodies of fish, birds, and animals and make them sick. In order to solve these issues, individuals, companies, and governments all need to take action.

Some people might argue that the actions of individual people will not affect plastic waste much. In my view, however, people can definitely help if they follow the "Three Rs." First, they should reduce how much plastic they use. They can buy products that come in glass or metal, not plastic. Second, people can reuse plastic products. Large plastic bottles are perfect for storing things, for example. Third, people can recycle plastic products.

Companies can also help solve the problem of plastic waste. They could make products from other materials, such as glass or metal, instead of plastic. They could stop using plastic to wrap the items they make. In my experience, many things that people buy have a lot of excess plastic around them, so this approach would definitely reduce plastic waste.

Finally, governments can help deal with the issue of plastic waste. They could encourage companies and individuals to use less plastic. They could ban plastic shopping bags and require stores to charge a small fee for paper ones. And governments could raise taxes for companies that use a lot of plastic and reduce taxes for companies that use other materials.

In conclusion, plastic waste is a serious and growing problem, but if individuals, companies, and governments all take action, this situation could definitely be improved.

B ANALYZE THE MODEL Match the paragraphs (a–c) to where the information appears in the model essay.

a. introductory paragraph   b. body paragraph   c. concluding paragraph

1. _____ A thesis statement that mentions who needs to solve the plastic waste issue

2. _____ An opinion about whether the problem can be solved

3. _____ An explanation of two reasons why plastic waste is an environmental issue

4. _____ Supporting ideas and details for the thesis statement

5. _____ A restatement of the thesis statement

WRITING SKILL   Organize a problem-solution essay

In a problem-solution essay, you describe one or more problems and suggest ways to solve them. These essays often have a block structure:

▸ An **introduction** that describes the problem. The thesis statement mentions how the problem can be solved and/or who needs to solve it.

▸ Two or more **body paragraphs**. Each body paragraph should have a topic sentence that relates to the thesis. The body paragraphs can each describe a different solution to the problem.

▸ A **concluding paragraph** that sums up the main ideas. It can also include an opinion of which solution or solutions are the most effective.

C APPLY Complete the outline of the body paragraphs of the model.

I. Individuals can help:

3 Rs—[1]_____, _____, _____

II. Companies can solve the problem of plastic waste:

Make products from [2]_____

Stop using [3]_____

III. Governments can help, too:

Encourage people to use [4]_____

Ban [5]_____

Raise [6]_____

A recycling station in Huaibei, China

D Complete the paragraph with a phrase from the box. Three phrases are extra.

another reason	obvious thing	sun's heat
tropical climates	the atmosphere	these devices
major cause	special clothes	traditional ways

Air conditioners are popular, especially in ¹_____, because they make life more comfortable. However, ²_____ can also contribute to environmental problems. For one thing, they require a lot of power to run, and generating power is one ³_____ of climate change. For another thing, air conditioners use a gas called freon to cool air. If this gas escapes into ⁴_____, it can trap the ⁵_____. Gases like freon are ⁶_____ why air conditioners can lead to climate change.

GRAMMAR Pronouns and related words

You use pronouns to refer to nouns that were mentioned before, or to nouns that are known. The most familiar pronouns are personal and possessive pronouns such as *I, you, he, him, she, her, it, they, them, mine, yours, his, hers,* and *theirs.*

We also use:

▶ (adjective +) *one/ones* as pronouns:
  *They should ban plastic bags and charge a small fee for **paper ones**.*

▶ *this/that/these/those* (+ noun phrase) to refer back to an idea or entire sentence:
  *Air conditioners release excess heat outside. **This** raises outdoor temperatures.*

Common mistakes with pronouns and related words include:

▶ not using the right pronoun

  ~~Her~~ **She** works hard.
  *Air conditioners make life more comfortable. ~~It~~ **This** is especially true in hot climates.*

▶ not agreeing with the noun

  ~~These~~ **This** idea was clear.
  ~~That~~ **Those** suggestions were helpful.

▶ using a pronoun when it is not clear which word the pronoun refers to

  *Scientists have developed three proposals. ~~They are helpful.~~ **The proposals** are helpful.*

E GRAMMAR Review the model essay. Find and underline the following items. Then circle the noun or noun phrase it refers to.

1. A personal pronoun in the introductory paragraph

2. A personal pronoun in body paragraph 1

3. *this* + noun phrase that replaces a noun in the concluding paragraph

F GRAMMAR Complete the sentences. More than one answer may be correct.

it	them	these things	they	this work

1. Many people think recycling is a great way to help the environment. However, some studies show that _____ is not actually a very effective approach.

2. Some people feel that farming, industry, and travel have had little effect on the climate. In contrast, other people feel that _____ have definitely had a major impact.

3. Clothes are often cheap. As a result, some people buy many items of clothing but throw _____ away after wearing _____ just a few times.

4. In 1962, Rachel Carson wrote a book called *Silent Spring*. _____ had a big impact on how people thought about the environment.

G GRAMMAR Replace the underlined phrases with a pronoun or related phrase.

1. Greta Thunberg is a young woman who is trying to protect the environment. <u>Greta Thunberg</u> convinced many people around the world to take action to achieve <u>the goal of protecting the environment</u>.

2. Surprisingly, smartphones, tablets, and laptops may be bad for the planet for several reasons. One reason is that making <u>smartphones, tablets, and laptops</u> requires a lot of power.

3. Geothermal energy is one kind of renewable energy. <u>Geothermal energy</u> is a good source of power in countries that have many volcanoes. <u>Countries with a lot of volcanoes</u> include Iceland, Italy, and Japan.

H EDIT Correct five mistakes with pronouns and related words.

There are many reasons why the clothing industry is not environmentally friendly. First, this industry uses a lot of water and chemicals to make clothes. This chemicals can lead to a lot of water pollution. Using and polluting water are bad because people and animals need them, too. Another reason is that the clothing industry uses a lot of power to make clothes. These causes a lot of CO_2 to enter the atmosphere, which can make the climate crisis worse. Finally, many clothes are made from a kind of plastic. When people wash or throw they away, this plastic can get into the environment where they can hurt people and animals.

PLAN & WRITE

I **BRAINSTORM** Follow the steps.

1. Choose an environmental problem to write about.

   ☐ climate change   ☐ pollution from cars   ☐ plastic
   ☐ pollution from factories   ☐ noise pollution   ☐ light pollution

2. Make notes about the problem and its effects.

   _____

   _____

   _____

   _____

3. Brainstorm possible solutions, then add notes to the chart.

	Solutions
What can individuals do?	
What can companies do?	
What can other organizations do?	
Other ideas?	

4. Highlight two or three solutions that you would like to write about.

WRITING TIP

In general, do not use a pronoun or related word to refer to a noun in an earlier paragraph. Also avoid using a pronoun if there's a chance that some of your readers may not understand what noun it refers to. In both cases, it's preferable to repeat the noun.

J OUTLINE Use the ideas from activity I to write an outline in your notebook. Follow the structure below.

Introductory paragraph

Background information

Description of the problem

Thesis statement

First body paragraph

One solution

Second body paragraph

Another solution

Concluding paragraph

Summary

Concluding idea

K FIRST DRAFT Use your outline to write a first draft of your problem-solution essay.

L REVISE Use this list as you write your second draft.

☐ Does your essay have a clear thesis statement?

☐ Does it follow a clear organization?

☐ Are the problem and its effects clearly described?

☐ Are the solutions clear?

☐ Is there any information that is not needed?

M EDIT Use this list as you write your final draft.

☐ Does your essay use pronouns and related words effectively?

☐ Are there any spelling or punctuation errors?

☐ Have all grammar mistakes been fixed?

N FINAL DRAFT Reread your essay and correct any errors. Then submit it to your teacher.

REFLECT

A Check (✓) the Reflect activities you can do and the academic skills you can use.

- ☐ consider the impact of inventions
- ☐ discuss the pros and cons of "green" actions
- ☐ consider what makes a solution innovative
- ☐ evaluate innovations
- ☐ write a problem-solution essay about an environmental issue

- ☐ understand references within a text
- ☐ organize a problem-solution essay
- ☐ pronouns and related words
- ☐ evaluate solutions

B Write the vocabulary words from the unit in the correct column. Add any other words that you learned. Circle words you still need to practice.

NOUN	VERB	ADJECTIVE	ADVERB & OTHER

C Reflect on the ideas in the unit as you answer these questions.

1. In general, do you think people are doing a good job of helping our planet?

   _____

   _____

2. Did anything you read cause you to want to change your behavior? What was it, and what would you change?

   _____

   _____

3. What is the most important thing you learned in this unit?

   _____

   _____

UNIT
6 | SAVVY SHOPPERS

Shopping at a bazaar, or market, Bahrain

IN THIS UNIT

▸ Consider what customers want

▸ Evaluate your shopping experiences

▸ Compare shopping habits

▸ Synthesize ideas about buyers and sellers

▸ Write a review of a product or service

SKILLS

READING
Recognize coherence and cohesion

WRITING
Organize a review

GRAMMAR
Comparatives, *as ... as*, superlatives

CRITICAL THINKING
Understand the order of events

CONNECT TO THE TOPIC

1. *Savvy* means "smart." Does this shopper seem like a savvy shopper?

2. If you had to use one word to describe your feelings about shopping, what word would you use, and why?

VOTE WITH YOUR WALLET

Reusable grocery bags at a natural and organic foods grocery store, California, USA

A Watch the video without sound. Work with a partner. Use these words to write a short description of what you saw. ▶ 6.1

buy	consumer	energy	environment	oceans
planet	pollution	product	shopping	trees

B Watch the video again, this time with sound. How closely does your description from activity A match the words you heard? ▶ 6.1

C Discuss the questions in a small group.

1. What do you think "your purchase makes a difference" and "vote with your wallet" mean?

2. Describe a time when you voted with your wallet. Do you feel that your purchase made a difference?

PREPARE TO READ

A VOCABULARY Read the sentences. Write the words in bold next to their definitions.

▸ Customers sometimes write an online **review** of a product after they buy it. Some people leave negative comments when they're not **satisfied**. Do you ever do this?

▸ Some people think positive reviews are not **trustworthy** because real customers didn't write them. They think these reviews are **fake**. What do you think?

▸ Some companies do not sell **goods**, such as manufactured products. Instead, they provide **services**, such as financial advice. Which do you buy more often: goods or services?

▸ Most businesses have **competitors**. Many people believe competition is good for customers. Do you think the **pressure** of competition is a good thing for consumers?

▸ The **majority** of companies sell goods and services online these days. It's likely that **in the long term** consumers will buy everything online. Would you only want to buy things online?

1. _____ (adj) able to be trusted; believable

2. _____ (adj) not real

3. _____ (adj) pleased because something is good

4. _____ (n) a written opinion about the quality of something

5. _____ (n) in business, companies with similar products and customers

6. _____ (n) products that a company sells

7. _____ (n) the act of influencing someone to do something

8. _____ (n) the largest number among a group of people or things

9. _____ (n) actions to help or do work for someone

10. _____ (phr) for a long period of time in the future

B PERSONALIZE Discuss the questions in activity A with a partner. Support your opinions.

REFLECT   Consider what customers want.

You are going to read about how some companies try to attract customers. Consider what matters to you when you buy goods or services. Add one more idea to the list below. Then rank the ideas in order from most important (1) to least important (6). Share your ideas in a small group.

When I buy something, I want it to be . . .

_____ environmentally friendly.   _____ inexpensive.

_____ of the highest quality.   _____ the latest version.

_____ delivered quickly.   _____ Other: _____.

READ

KEEPING CUSTOMERS HAPPY

🎧 6.1

1   Many of us enjoy shopping. We enjoy going to stores or getting a delivery, opening the box, and being able to try the product. Usually, we're happy with the **goods** and **services** we purchase, but sometimes there's a problem and we're not **satisfied**. Why? Some of the reasons may be in what companies are doing behind the scenes[1] to get your business.

2   If you're like the **majority** of people, you read online **reviews** before you purchase something. Otherwise, it's hard to know the quality of something before you buy it. One study suggests that positive reviews influence about 90 percent of consumers. Companies know this, and many of them feel **pressure** to have positive reviews of their products. That's hard to achieve, though. A small mistake can make a customer unhappy and lead to a bad review. Most businesses understand there's little they can do about this situation except to try to give every customer a great experience. But some businesses take a different approach. They pay for **fake** reviews to try to attract customers. One consumer organization claims that almost 15 percent of reviews on one popular travel website may be fake. In the short term, fake reviews can benefit a company. However, **in the long term**, the company will probably suffer because customers will be unhappy if the quality of what they receive is not what they expect.

---

[1]**behind the scenes** (phr) privately; not in the open

A PREVIEW Look at the title and photo and read the caption. Why do you think the oil tanks are decorated with cartoons?

T 205

An oil tank decorated with cartoon fish sits near wind turbines in Amsterdam, the Netherlands.

3   Most people want to pay a low price for the goods and services they need. Companies know this. As a result, there's always pressure on them to reduce their prices. Because lower prices mean lower profits, there is a limit to how much companies can cut their prices. But some companies are able to go below this limit. One reason they can do this is because they make extra money by selling their customers' private data to advertisers. These companies are then able to offer more attractive prices on products and services than their **competitors**. This in turn helps them increase their market share[2]. However, 90 percent of consumers say they are unlikely to buy from companies that don't protect customer data. Businesses that sell customers' data to make money may find that doing this actually costs them money in the long-term.

4   A growing number of consumers are choosing products that protect the environment rather than harm it. One survey suggests that around 9 in 10 consumers trust companies that support the environment. Some companies sell goods that are difficult to make environmentally friendly and simply accept their situation. But others practice something called "greenwashing." Greenwashing means claiming[3] or suggesting that a product is better for the environment than it really is. For example, a business might call its product "Nature-Plus" even though that product is not natural at all. Greenwashing can benefit a company's sales in the short term. But if customers find out, there may be a backlash[4] which can affect profits. For example, when a major oil company advertised that it helps protect the environment, thousands of people—including Greta Thunberg—protested. This is because the oil industry is not always known to be environmentally friendly.

5   Most businesses are responsible and **trustworthy**. Still, consumers need to be aware that businesses do pay for fake reviews, sell customer data, or greenwash. Part of the reason is that all companies are under pressure to make a profit. This pressure can cause some companies to make very different choices about how to attract and keep customers. The good news is that through pressure from customers, more companies are aware that hurting consumers also hurts them.

---

[2]**market share** (n phr) how much one company sells compared to its competitors

[3]**claim** (v) to state that something is true

[4]**backlash** (n) a strong negative reaction by people

B MAIN IDEAS Complete each main idea statement with a phrase below (a–d). One phrase is extra.

a. want "green" products   c. accept that their personal data is sold

b. buy cheap, low-quality goods   d. don't always trust reviews

1. Customers _____ because some companies pay people to write only positive comments.

2. Some customers _____ so that some businesses can keep their prices very low.

3. Customers _____, so some companies falsely say they are environmentally friendly.

C **MAIN IDEAS** Complete the sentence about the main idea of the reading.

A company may benefit in the short term but may lose business in _____ if it uses bad business practices to attract customers.

D **DETAILS** Scan the reading to find the answers. Write the paragraph numbers where you find them.

1. _____ How many people seem to be influenced by good reviews?

2. _____ How many people want companies to protect their data?

3. _____ How many reviews on one site might not be real?

4. _____ What product name might be attractive to consumers?

5. _____ How many consumers trust companies that care about the environment?

6. _____ Who protested against greenwashing?

E **DETAILS** Write the answers to the questions in activity D.

1. _____

2. _____

3. _____

4. _____

5. _____

6. _____

READING SKILL   Recognize coherence and cohesion

An article has **coherence** when the paragraphs are organized in a way that makes sense, such as chronologically. In an article with **cohesion**, the links between sentences and ideas are easy to understand. These links are sometimes shown with words and phrases, such as *on the other hand*, *as a result*, and *next*. Other times the connection is made with pronouns. For example, notice how the pronouns help link ideas in these two sentences:

*One study suggests that positive reviews influence about 90 percent of consumers. Companies know **this**, and many of **them** feel pressure to have positive reviews of **their** products.*

Recognizing coherence and cohesion can help you follow a writer's ideas and arguments. It will also help your writing.

F **APPLY** Choose the best place to add each sentence to the article.

1. *As a result, they might leave negative reviews of their own.*

   a. at the end of paragraph 2   b. at the end of paragraph 3

2. *How much of a problem is this?*

   a. before "One consumer organization claims . . ." in paragraph 2

   b. before "However, in the long term . . ." in paragraph 2

3. *In fact, a survey showed that customers' feelings about prices were a huge worry for many businesses.*

   a. before "Because lower prices mean . . ." in paragraph 3

   b. before "One reason they can do this is because they make . . ." in paragraph 3

G APPLY Put the events (a–d) in the order that they must have happened in each paragraph.

1. Paragraph 2

   a. _____ A company pays for fake reviews.

   b. _____ A customer is not satisfied.

   c. _____ A customer makes a purchase.

   d. _____ A customer reads a review.

2. Paragraph 4

   a. _____ A company decides to greenwash.

   b. _____ A customer becomes unhappy.

   c. _____ A company wants more customers

   d. _____ A customer learns about the greenwashing.

REFLECT   Evaluate your shopping experiences.

Write answers to the questions. Then share your ideas with a group.

1. Have you had any experiences like the ones in the reading *Keeping Customers Happy*? If so, explain.

   _____

2. What's the most positive shopping experience with a company that you've ever had?

   _____

A satisfied customer

PREPARE TO READ

A VOCABULARY Read the questions. Write the words in bold next to their definitions.

1. Do you believe that **financial** success is important?
2. If you find money, is it **ethical** to keep it?
3. If you want to research or **investigate** the quality of a product, what do you do?
4. In general, do you think that the pros of social media **outweigh** the cons?
5. What **criteria** can help you decide where to go for a vacation?
6. What kinds of goals do you **set** for yourself?
7. When a product breaks, do you replace it or ask someone to **fix** it?
8. Did (or do) your parents offer any **incentive** to get you to study hard?
9. Which is your idea of **paradise**: a day by yourself or a day with friends?
10. How might a restaurant try to stop customer satisfaction from **declining**?

1. _____ (v) to go down or to get worse

2. _____ (adj) relating to correct and acceptable behavior

3. _____ (n) a situation or place that is perfect

4. _____ (n) something that encourages a person to do something

5. _____ (n) things or reasons that help you choose

6. _____ (v) to be more important

7. _____ (v) to examine something carefully

8. _____ (v) to repair something that is broken

9. _____ (v) to give; to make

10. _____ (adj) relating to money

B PERSONALIZE Discuss five of the questions from activity A with a partner.

REFLECT   Compare shopping habits.

> Choose the word that makes each statement true for you. Discuss your reasons in a small group.
>
> 1. I **often / sometimes / never** feel happy when I buy a new product.
> 2. I **often / sometimes / never** buy things that I don't really need.
> 3. I **often / sometimes / never** spend too much money when I shop online.
> 4. I **often / sometimes / never** make a list before I go shopping.
> 5. I **often / sometimes / never** research a product before I buy it.

BE A **BETTER BUYER**

🎧 6.2

1   For some of us, the world is a consumer **paradise**. We can purchase more goods and services at lower prices than ever before. We can shop whenever we want, buy whatever we want, and have it delivered wherever we want. But is it really a paradise to buy things just because they're easy to get, cheap, and convenient? Maybe not. In order to keep prices as low as possible, some companies cut costs in ways we may not agree with. They may not pay their workers enough, or they may make products that hurt the

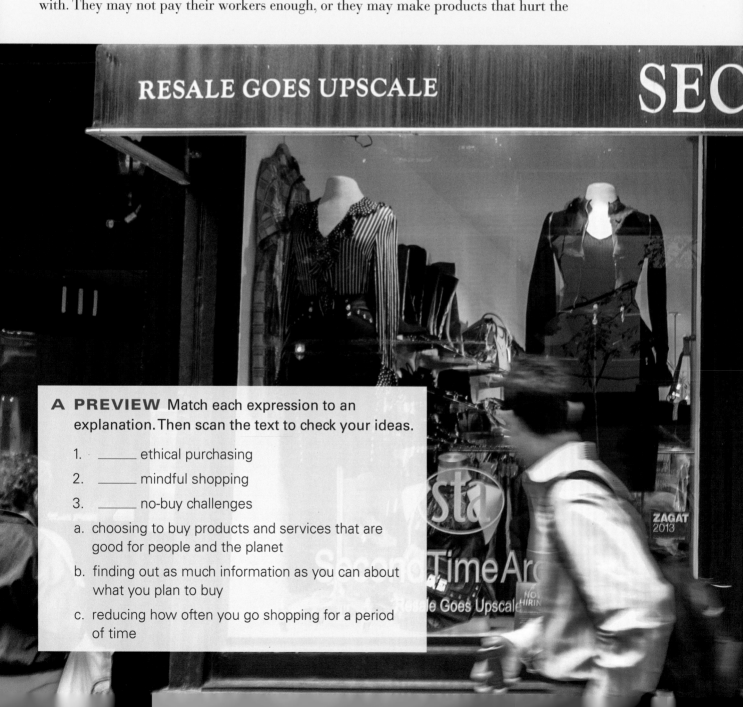

RESALE GOES UPSCALE

SEC

A PREVIEW Match each expression to an explanation. Then scan the text to check your ideas.

1. _____ ethical purchasing

2. _____ mindful shopping

3. _____ no-buy challenges

a. choosing to buy products and services that are good for people and the planet

b. finding out as much information as you can about what you plan to buy

c. reducing how often you go shopping for a period of time

environment. Cutting costs can lead to lower quality products, too. In fact, according to one study, 66 percent of us feel that the quality of products has **declined** recently. Fortunately, there are ways that consumers can make a difference.

2   **Ethical** purchasing may be one way to help the situation. Ethical consumers buy products that meet certain **criteria**. For example, one consumer might only buy clothes from companies that care for the environment. Another person might only buy goods made by businesses that treat their workers well. Shopping ethically requires some work. Consumers have to research or **investigate** which goods and companies meet their criteria. Although ethically made items can be expensive, the advantages of this approach **outweigh** the negatives. Ethical approaches to business lead to a positive cycle that benefits everybody. Businesses have strong **incentives** to care for the environment and for their workers because both things attract customers. Consumers can feel confident that when they shop for clothes and other items, they're helping society and the planet.

A second-hand clothing store in Soho, New York, USA

3   Mindful shopping is another way to be a better buyer. Mindful consumers try not to make impulse purchases[1]. Instead, they think before they buy. Mindful shopping can be as basic as making a shopping list and getting only the things on the list. At a deeper level, mindful shopping involves thinking carefully about what to buy and whether to buy it. Consumers might ask themselves whether they really need a new pair of jeans. They might decide to buy vintage, or second-hand, goods instead of something new. Alternatively, they might decide to buy only higher-quality but more expensive new items. This may be better than buying lower-quality products that are likely to wear out quickly. Better-quality goods are generally more expensive, so this approach may cost more in the short term. In the long term, though, these consumers may save money because their clothes and other items will last longer.

4   A final step we can take is more radical[2]. We can simply stop shopping. "No-buy challenges" are popular on social media and can help people end the cycle of spend, spend, spend. The idea is simple: A consumer decides to buy as little as possible for a certain period of time. One person, for example, might **set** herself the challenge of only buying fruit and vegetables for a week. Another person might add *one* treat, like ice cream, to his list and do it for a month. Some people set no-buy challenges for a year, or even longer! It may seem impossible not to buy things for this long, especially clothes. But items can be **fixed** instead of replaced. Other items can be borrowed or exchanged. It's not easy to complete a no-buy challenge; however, people who have tried and succeeded feel that the experience has changed their lives in positive ways.

5   The convenience of modern shopping not only affects our **financial** health—because we spend too much—but also influences our idea of happiness. Ethical purchasing, mindful shopping, and no-buy challenges offer ways to make our world a cleaner, healthier, and happier place—in other words, a true consumer paradise.

---

[1]**impulse purchase** (n phr) something you buy without thinking much about your decision
[2]**radical** (adj) different from the way things have been traditionally done

B MAIN IDEAS Choose the correct answers.

1. What is the main idea of the article?

   a. Consumers can do several things to make shopping better for them and the planet.

   b. The world is more of a paradise for companies and consumers than it used to be.

2. What is the purpose of paragraph 2?

   a. To contrast ethical purchasing with other ways consumers can shop

   b. To explain what ethical purchasing is and how consumers can do it

3. What is the main idea of paragraph 3?

   a. Consumers like mindful shopping because it is easy for them to do.

   b. Mindful shopping can help consumers shop better and spend less.

4. What does the writer say about no-buy challenges in paragraph 4?

   a. Although they are simple to understand, many people find them hard to do.

   b. They have a small impact on people despite being simple to understand.

C DETAILS Write T for *True* or F for *False* for each statement. Add the paragraph number where the information can be found. Then correct each false statement to make it true.

1. _____ Items that have been made in an ethical way can be more expensive than other items. (paragraph _____)

2. _____ Mindful shoppers who buy high-quality items might spend less in the long-term. (paragraph _____)

3. _____ A study showed that about one-third of people felt goods had gone down in quality. (paragraph _____)

4. _____ Shopping can have an emotional effect as well as a financial impact on consumers. (paragraph _____)

5. _____ The period of a typical no-buy challenge can be anything between a week and a month. (paragraph _____)

D DETAILS Decide which paragraph (paragraph 2, 3 or 4) each detail can be added to. Then indicate (^) the best place in the paragraph to add the detail. Compare your answers with a partner.

a. _____ They might wait 24 hours between deciding to get something and actually buying it.

b. _____ And somebody who *really* wants a challenge might buy nothing at all for 10 days.

c. _____ This is because they usually cost more to make since workers are paid better.

REFLECT Synthesize ideas about buyers and sellers.

Both articles in this unit focus on companies and consumers. Check (✓) whether each idea is mentioned in the first article, the second article, or both. Compare your answers with a partner.

Ideas	Keeping Customers Happy	Be a Better Buyer
1. Companies that don't act in ethical ways may eventually harm themselves.		
2. Consumers can benefit if they stop buying things for a time.		
3. Not all online comments can be trusted.		
4. Shopping can have a negative impact on consumers.		
5. Some consumers care about buying "green" products.		
6. To keep costs down, companies sometimes have to make tough choices.		
7. Smart consumers can help make businesses more responsible.		

WRITE

Assembling sneakers,
Lawrence, Massachusetts, USA

UNIT TASK Write a review of a product or service.

You are going to write a review of a product that you've purchased or a service that you've used. Your purpose is to help others make smart choices. Use the ideas, vocabulary, and skills from the unit.

A MODEL Read the review. Choose the correct word to complete each statement.

1. The writer reviewed a **product / service**.
2. The writer's overall opinion is **positive / negative**.

A Review of My Sneakers

Recently I was shopping online and I saw a pair of sneakers on sale. Usually I read reviews before I buy anything online. However, in this case, I just decided to buy them because I needed new sneakers, the price was low, and there was only one pair left in my size. On the whole, I'm glad I made that decision.

There are several things that I especially like about the shoes. First, they're really light. Compared with my old shoes, the new ones weigh about half as much. This means my legs feel less tired after a workout. In addition, they're better for the environment than other shoes. I didn't know this when I bought them, but they can apparently be recycled easily because they were made using a "cradle-to-cradle design process." The final good point is the price. I got them for just $72, and good sneakers are usually not as cheap as that. In fact, it's probably the best price I've ever paid for quality shoes.

Although I like the shoes a lot, there are two things that I find less appealing. First, the shoes are not as stylish as I would like. They have a really bright, colorful design, but I would prefer a simpler style and darker colors. Because the design is so bright, people often ask me where I got them. At first, I thought this was funny, but it's becoming more frustrating now because it happens almost all the time. Second, I was disappointed that the shoes were wrapped in plastic inside the box. These shoes are supposed to be good for the planet, so I feel the plastic wasn't needed.

Overall, the shoes are great, and I definitely recommend them. In fact, I'm going to buy another pair, though I'll look for a less colorful pair next time!

Shopping for sneakers, Paris, France

WRITING SKILL   Organize a review

Writing a review involves elements of other kinds of writing. These include expressing opinions, describing things, discussing problems, and comparing pros and cons. When you write a review, you can organize your ideas into four paragraphs.

Introductory paragraph
Describe what you are reviewing and give some background information. You can also explain briefly how you know about the product or service.

Body paragraph 1
Introduce up to three strengths (good points) of the product or service. For each point, add supporting details or examples.

Body paragraph 2
Introduce up to three weaknesses (bad points) of the product or service. For each point, add supporting details or examples.

Concluding paragraph
State your overall opinion about the product or service. You can also give a recommendation about whether other people should buy it or not.

B ANALYZE THE MODEL Look at the model. Underline the following.

1. Background information that the writer gives in the introductory paragraph

2. Three strengths of the product that the writer mentions in the first body paragraph

3. Examples from the second body paragraph that support the writer's opinion that the shoes are not very stylish or good for the environment

4. The overall opinion that the writer gives in the concluding paragraph

C APPLY Use the notes in the T-chart to complete the review of a phone. Write complete sentences.

Weaknesses	Strengths
Slow ➔ can't use apps I like	Cheap ➔ just $99
Battery lasts eight hrs. ➔ last phone was better	Bright and clear screen ➔ easy to see even in the sun
Heavy ➔ get tired if hold too long	Good photos ➔ lots of features (e.g., filters)

There are three main issues with this phone. First, it's very slow. As a result,

¹_____. Second, ²_____.

My last phone had a much better battery. Finally, it's heavier than I expected. Therefore,

³_____. The phone does have some good points.

For one thing, it wasn't very expensive. In fact, ⁴_____. Second,

⁵_____. I can even read it easily when I'm outside on

a sunny day. In addition, it has a good camera. ⁶_____.

GRAMMAR Comparatives, *as . . . as*, superlatives

Comparative adjectives

Comparative adjectives describe nouns. We use them to show that one thing is different from another. Use adjective + *-er* (+ *than*) with one-syllable and some two-syllable adjectives. With longer adjectives, use *more/less* + adjective (+ *than*).

> This book is **easier/more expensive** (**than** that book).

Comparative adverbs

Comparative adverbs describe verbs. They follow the same rules as comparative adjectives.

> The computer works **faster/more efficiently than** we expected.

as . . . as

To show how two things are the same or not, use (*not*) *as* + adjective/adverb + *as*.

> This television is **as cheap as** other TVs in the store.
>
> This phone does **not** ring **as loudly as** my other one.

Superlatives

We use superlative adjectives and adverbs to compare one thing with many things. Use *the* + adjective/adverb + *-est* with one-syllable words and some two-syllable adjectives. With longer adjectives and adverbs that end in *-ly*, use *the most/the least* + adjective/adverb. Note that there are some irregular forms (e.g., *the best*, *the worst*).

> In my opinion, it is one of **the best/the worst** companies (in the world).
>
> Among all the packages, this one was delivered **the most quickly/the most slowly**.

D GRAMMAR Complete the sentences with the correct form of the word in parentheses.

1. Computers today work _____ (quickly) ones from five years ago.

2. Don't buy _____ (expensive) television in the store.

3. My new neighborhood isn't _____ (pretty) my old one.

4. Let's go to this restaurant. It has _____ (efficient) service than the other one.

E GRAMMAR In your notebook, write one or two sentences about each topic. Use comparatives, *(not) as . . . as*, or superlatives. Then share your sentences with a partner.

1. two foods

    _____

2. the best gift you have ever received

    _____

3. a person who is different from you in some way

    _____

4. the least favorite thing you have to do each week

    _____

5. two things or people that are as good as each other

    _____

F EDIT Correct the six mistakes with comparatives, *(not) as . . . as*, or superlatives in this paragraph.

I wanted to save money because I spent the more than I planned at the end of last year. So I decided to do a no-buy challenge for two weeks. I allowed myself to buy fruit and vegetables only. I told some friends about my plan, and they decided to do it, too. On the whole, the experience was better I expected. The first few days were the most hardest because my habit was to go shopping every day. The next few days were as not as difficult, and after a week it became much easier. In fact, I had more free time than before, so my life was actually the best than it used to be. I saved money too, but less than I was expecting. Still, it was a very good experience. Most of my friends felt that the experience was as positive as I did, and several of us have decided to continue our no-buy challenges for more longer.

Vegetables for sale, Perekrestok Supermarket, Moscow, Russia

PLAN & WRITE

G BRAINSTORM Complete the chart with some products you have bought or services you have used. Add strengths and weaknesses with supporting details.

Product or service	Strengths	Weaknesses

H PLAN Complete the steps.

1. Decide which product or service you will write about in your review.

2. Decide which strengths, weaknesses, and supporting details you will mention and in which order.

3. Decide what overall opinion about the product or service you will give.

WRITING TIP

When you're brainstorming, planning, or writing an outline, it's OK to take notes in your language. However, when you write in English, it's a good idea to use full sentences because this will help you become more confident about writing.

I OUTLINE Review the Writing Skill box and write an outline for your review.

Introductory paragraph

Background information: _____

Product or service: _____

Body paragraph 1

Main points: _____

Details: _____

Body paragraph 2

Main points: _____

Details: _____

Concluding paragraph

Overall opinion: _____

J FIRST DRAFT Use your outline to write a first draft of your review.

K REVISE Use this list as you write your second draft.

☐ Does your review have an introduction, body paragraphs, and conclusion?

☐ Does it follow a clear, logical organization (i.e., does it have coherence and cohesion)?

☐ Is your overall opinion about the product or service clear?

☐ Have you supported your points with reasons, details, or examples?

L EDIT Use this list as you write your final draft.

☐ Does your review include comparatives, *(not) as . . . as*, and/or superlatives?

☐ Have you fixed any grammar mistakes?

M FINAL DRAFT Reread your review and correct any errors. Then submit it to your teacher.

Shopping center,
Bangkok, Thailand

REFLECT

A Check (✓) the Reflect activities you can do and the academic skills you can use.

☐ consider what customers want

☐ evaluate your shopping experiences

☐ compare shopping habits

☐ synthesize ideas about buyers and sellers

☐ write a review of a product or service

☐ recognize coherence and cohesion

☐ organize a review

☐ comparatives, *as . . . as*, superlatives

☐ understand the order of events

B Write the vocabulary words from the unit in the correct column. Add any other words that you learned. Circle words you still need to practice.

NOUN	VERB	ADJECTIVE	ADVERB & OTHER

C Reflect on the ideas in the unit as you answer these questions.

1. What was the most interesting thing you learned from this unit?

   _____

   _____

2. Will you change your shopping habits after studying this unit? Explain.

   _____

   _____

3. How do you think shopping will change in the future?

   _____

   _____

UNIT
7 | WHO WE ARE,
HOW WE ACT

A diver touches a great white shark on the nose, Guadalupe Island, Mexico.

IN THIS UNIT

▶ Compare and contrast personality types

▶ Consider your behavior in different situations

▶ Evaluate reasons why people help others

▶ Consider the effects of cognitive biases

▶ Write a compare-contrast essay about experiences

SKILLS

READING
Recognize cause and effect

WRITING
Organize a compare-contrast essay

GRAMMAR
Compare-and-contrast connectors

CRITICAL THINKING
Connect information to personal experiences

CONNECT TO THE TOPIC

1. What words might describe the person touching the shark in the photo?
2. Would you enjoy doing what the people in the photograph are doing?

WATCH

CAKES OF DECEPTION

A You are going to watch a video about an experiment with cakes. Watch the first part of the video and complete the summary. ▶ 7.1

birthday	camera	taste	$15	$40	$55

In the experiment, a hidden ¹_____ will watch people to see whether the price of something can affect its ²_____. Random people will have a chance to try two different cakes. The first one costs ³_____. The other cake costs ⁴_____. The people who try the cakes will be asked what they think about them.

B Predict the answer to each statement. Then watch the whole video to confirm your ideas. ▶ 7.2

1. The majority of people who tried the first cake said that it was
   a. dry and a little bit disappointing.   b. more delicious than they expected.

2. The general opinion about the second cake was that it tasted
   a. about the same as the first cake.   b. a lot better than the first cake.

3. To make the experiment more interesting, the two cakes
   a. were actually exactly the same.   b. were made with different ingredients.

4. The experiment suggested that many people think that
   a. a high price is a sign of good quality.   b. there is no link between price and taste.

5. Overall, most people who tried the two cakes were surprised
   a. that the two cakes were so similar.   b. when they learned the truth.

C Discuss the questions in a small group.

1. How do you think you would have reacted to the two cakes?

2. Do you agree that price can affect how we react to products?

PREPARE TO READ

A VOCABULARY Read the sentences. Then choose the correct definition for each bold word.

1. Someone who is **outgoing** likes to be with and talk to other people.

    a. shy and quiet
    b. friendly and sociable

2. **Reserved** people tend to enjoy being alone and being quiet.

    a. open about one's views
    b. private about one's views

3. If you look at a bright light and then shut your eyes, the brightness **persists** for a time.

    a. continues
    b. changes

4. Many people find that relaxing at home is a good way to **recharge** their batteries.

    a. to rest and gain energy
    b. to be active and use energy

5. People with the **desire** to take risks often enjoy activities such as snowboarding or diving.

    a. strong wish or hope
    b. strong interest in winning

6. **Qualities** such as leadership and creativity are valued in businesses.

    a. effects
    b. characteristics

7. It's **inaccurate** to say that Canada is cold in winter; some parts of the country have relatively mild weather.

    a. not known
    b. not correct

8. Some people are **comfortable** talking to strangers; others find it very difficult.

    a. relaxed; at ease
    b. not happy; not ready

9. It isn't good to **label** children as "smart" or "lazy" because such terms can affect them.

    a. to learn or teach
    b. to name or describe

10. Young children are often very **energetic**, which can be tiring for their parents.

    a. full of energy
    b. having little energy

REFLECT Compare and contrast personality types.

Before you read an article about personality types, consider two well-known types: *introvert*, or someone who generally likes to spend time alone, and *extrovert*, someone who typically enjoys being with other people. Complete the Venn diagram with the adjectives (a–h). Add two adjectives of your own. Compare your ideas in a small group.

Mainly introvert | **Both** | **Mainly extrovert**

| a. energetic | c. funny | e. loud | g. reserved | i. _____ |
| b. friendly | d. kind | f. outgoing | h. shy | j. _____ |

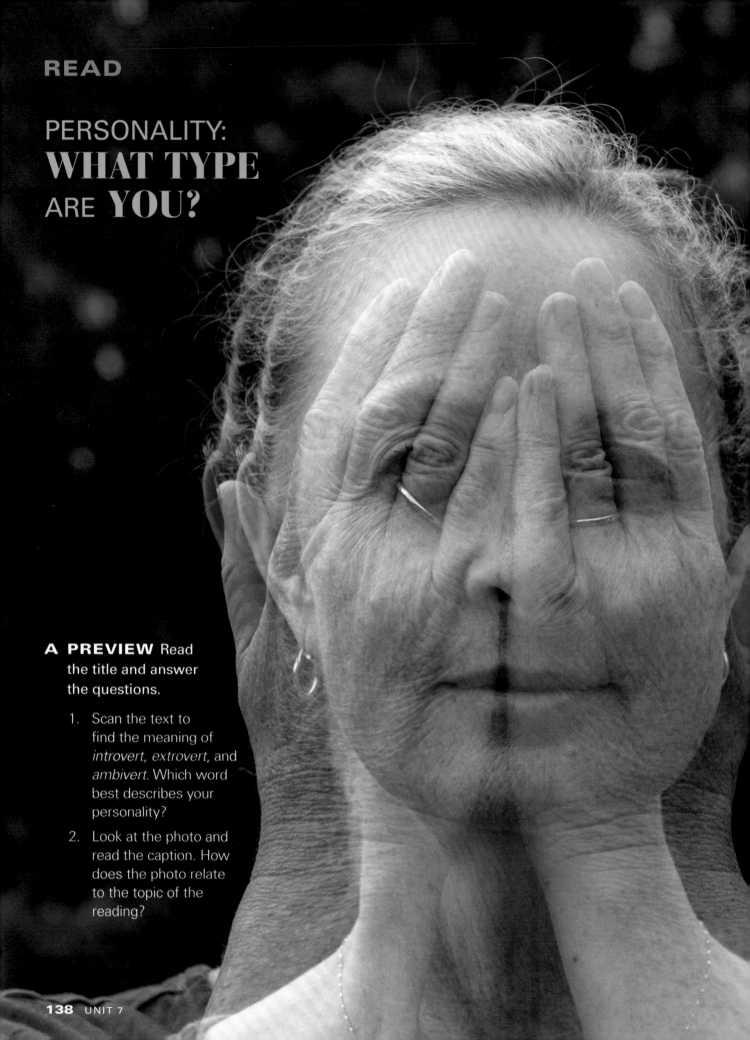

READ

PERSONALITY: **WHAT TYPE** ARE **YOU?**

A PREVIEW Read the title and answer the questions.

1. Scan the text to find the meaning of *introvert*, *extrovert*, and *ambivert*. Which word best describes your personality?

2. Look at the photo and read the caption. How does the photo relate to the topic of the reading?

1   Do you prefer being by yourself or with a lot of people? Are you usually quiet, or do you tend to talk a lot? Your answers will depend on your personality. For thousands of years, people have tried to understand and describe different personalities. Many of their ideas and descriptions were not very accurate. But the work of psychologist[1] Carl Jung in the early 1920s provided some clear answers. In particular, Jung was the first to describe two well-known personality traits[2]: introversion and extroversion.

2   According to Jung's theory, introverts are **reserved** people who like to think before they speak. They are **comfortable** spending time with close friends but dislike large crowds. In contrast, extroverts are typically **outgoing**. They're quick to act and enjoy spending time in groups. Later research suggested that introverts need time alone to **recharge**, but extroverts feel more **energetic** when they're with other people. These descriptions are easy to understand and widely accepted. They're also so well known that most people can say which term better describes them.

3   Although it is convenient to put things in two categories, current thinking is that we cannot rely on this simple classification. One problem with Jung's theory is that most people aren't simply either introverts or extroverts. The common understanding is that introversion and extroversion are separate types in the same way that black and white are separate colors. When it comes to personality, though, this understanding is **inaccurate**. This is because very few people are either completely introverted or extroverted. Instead, almost all of us have a certain amount of both traits. In fact, as many as two-thirds of us are neither introverts nor extroverts but something else: ambiverts.

4   Ambiverts act like both introverts and extroverts. They do this at different times and in different situations. An ambivert might enjoy hanging out with a large crowd of people one day and then wish for quiet time alone the next day. Ambiverts also combine the positive traits of both introversion and extroversion. Like introverts, they can be good listeners. Like extroverts, they are comfortable talking and expressing themselves. Another **quality** of ambiverts is that they can match their behavior to the situation. For example, an ambivert can make small talk[3] with an outgoing passenger on a train. Conversely, the same ambivert can recognize a reserved passenger's **desire** to sit quietly.

In this double exposure photograph, the photographer purposely recorded one image directly over another.

---

[1]**psychologist** (n) a person who studies human thinking and behavior
[2]**trait** (n) a quality, or characteristic, of somebody's personality or character
[3]**make small talk** (v phr) to talk about everyday topics, often with somebody you don't know well

5   So why does the idea that we're either introverts or extroverts **persist**? One reason is that our brains have developed certain ways of thinking. These ways are called cognitive biases[4]. Cognitive biases can affect how we understand information. One example is called "binary bias." This form of bias leads us to put information into a limited number of categories—often just two—instead of many. Because of this bias, people naturally see things as being either black or white instead of a shade[5] of gray. In other words, these two labels persist because our brains like to put things into just two categories.

6   **Labeling** someone an extrovert or introvert can do more than describe their personality. This label can actually change who they are. Imagine an ambivert girl growing up in a family of extroverts. The girl behaves in introverted ways more often than her parents, brother, and sister. As a result, people call her an introvert, and she grows up thinking that this label fits her. Over time, she learns to avoid situations and behaviors that are typical of extroverts. She prefers to be in smaller groups and to spend time alone. This is a second reason why the labels "introvert" and "extrovert" persist: People sometimes grow into patterns of behavior based on how they are labeled.

7   The next time someone asks if you're an introvert or extrovert, consider your answer carefully. Most personalities are more complex and cannot be easily labeled as one or the other.

---

[4]**cognitive bias** (n phr) an error in thinking caused by the brain trying to simplify information
[5]**shade** (n) a type of color

B MAIN IDEAS Choose the better heading for each paragraph.

Paragraph 2

a. The differences between two personality types

b. Two ways that personalities change over time

Paragraph 3

a. Problems with a widely accepted theory

b. A new but uncommon personality type

Paragraph 4

a. Good situations and bad ones

b. A mixed personality type

Paragraph 5

a. Why certain shades are easier to see

b. How thinking can affect understanding

Paragraph 6

a. The surprising impact that a label can have

b. The unusual impact that a family can have

C DETAILS Read each statement. Write T for *True*, F for *False,* or NG for *Not Given*.

1. _____ Carl Jung was the first person to describe the ambivert personality.

2. _____ Introverts and extroverts react differently to being with other people.

3. _____ Introversion and extroversion are separate things like black and white.

4. _____ Up to 66 percent of people may have an ambivert personality type.

5. _____ Most ambiverts usually act more like extroverts than introverts.

6. _____ The term "cognitive bias" describes some of the ways we think.

7. _____ A boy who calls himself an extrovert may become a more extroverted adult.

D DETAILS Complete the notes. Use two words from the article for each answer.

Introverts

Dislike [1]_____ but enjoy being with close friends

Need some [2]_____ to be able to recharge

Being [3]_____ is one of their positive qualities

Extroverts

First described by [4]_____ around 100 years ago

Outgoing, talkative, and like to hang out in [5]_____

Being with [6]_____ makes them have more energy

Ambiverts

Have a [7]_____ of both introverted and extroverted traits

Act differently at [8]_____ and in different situations

May find it comfortable to make [9]_____ with strangers

READING SKILL Recognize cause and effect

Causes are the reasons *why* certain things happen, and effects are *what* happens as a result of an event or situation. Recognizing cause and effect helps you better understand relationships between ideas, which is an important part of reading. Here are some connectors that signal cause and effect.

        cause   *effect*   *cause*   *effect*

cause-effect: It began to rain, **so** I went home. / It was raining. **As a result**, I went home.

        effect   *cause*   *effect*   *cause*

effect-cause: I went home **because** it started raining. / I went home **because of** the rain.

Because effects always happen after their causes, you should also look for expressions that signal the order in which events happened:

    effect   *cause*
Many people opened their umbrellas **after** the rain began.

E APPLY Circle the correct connector to complete these causes and effects described in the text.

1. A girl grows up thinking she is an introvert, **because / so** she learns to act in more introverted ways over time.

2. An ambivert acts in a more outgoing way **before / during** a conversation with an extrovert on public transportation.

3. An introvert spends time with a large group of people. **As a result, / The reason is** he or she feels a desire for some time alone.

4. An idea about personality types became familiar **after / so** Carl Jung described introversion and extroversion.

5. **Because / So** the "binary bias" affects how we think, our brains like to put information into just a few categories.

CRITICAL THINKING Connect information to personal experiences

You may understand an article better if you connect it to your personal experiences. Think about how your life experiences are similar to or different from the information in the article. Ask yourself questions that help you do this; for example, *Which personality type sounds more like me?* or *How is my personality similar to or different from other people in my family?*

REFLECT   Consider your behavior in different situations.

Answer the questions in your notebook. Then share your ideas in a small group.

1. How do you feel about spending time with large groups of people? How do you behave when you're in a group?

2. How do you feel about spending time alone? What do you usually do?

PREPARE TO READ

A VOCABULARY Read the definitions. Then complete each sentence with one or two bold words.

donate (v) to help by giving money, time, or goods to a person or charity
donor (n) a person who gives money or other things to a charity
funds (n) money for a specific purpose
operation (n) cutting open a person's body in order to fix a medical problem
pattern (n) the specific way that something is usually done or organized
persuade (v) to convince a person to do or believe something
reasonable (adj) appropriate
simplify (v) to make something easier to understand
sympathy (n) a feeling of sadness for someone's bad luck
take advantage of (v phr) to benefit from an event or situation

1. Every year, Canadians _____ more than $10 billion to charities, with each _____ giving $450 on average.

2. Great teachers can _____ complex ideas so they're easier to understand.

3. When it's sunny, many people go outdoors to _____ the nice weather.

4. Most people feel _____ for a friend who is in the hospital.

5. Some charities use the _____ they raise to provide clean water for people. Others use the money to help sick people who need a(n) _____.

6. To help a child develop a good sleep _____, set a _____ bedtime, such as 9 p.m., and wake him/her at the same time each morning.

7. The purpose of advertisements is to _____ people to buy goods or services.

B PERSONALIZE Discuss these questions with a partner.

1. In your opinion, what's a **reasonable** price for these items: a cup of coffee, a pizza, a phone?

2. In addition to bad luck, what other situations make you feel **sympathy** for others?

3. What kind of weather do you like best, and how do you **take advantage of** it?

REFLECT Evaluate reasons why people help others.

You're going to read about how charities try to raise money. Rank the reasons you think people donate to charities from most common (1) to least common (5). Make notes to support your views. Then compare your ideas in a small group.

People donate money, time, or goods to charities . . .

_____ after seeing friends or family make donations.
_____ because of a desire to help other people.
_____ because they feel it is the right thing to do.
_____ so they can feel good about themselves.
_____ to teach children that giving is important.

THE PSYCHOLOGY OF GIVING

🎧 7.2

1   Every year, people all over the world give hundreds of billions of dollars to charities¹. In 2017, for example, Americans **donated** $410 billion to charities. In terms of revenue², that's more than the second-largest company in the world. While some people are incredibly generous, many give rarely or never donate at all. As a result, charities are always looking for ways to encourage more people to donate. One way they do this is by **taking advantage of** human psychology—how people think and behave— and especially of our cognitive biases.

2   These biases are **patterns** of thinking that can influence how we understand, act, and decide. They typically affect our thinking by helping us make quick decisions based on limited information, or by **simplifying** a complex situation so we can understand it more easily. We're usually not aware of biases. In other words, we don't notice that they're affecting our thinking, and we can't easily control or reduce their effects.

3   One type of cognitive bias, called the "truth effect," makes short, simple stories easier to believe than longer, more complex ones. Some charities use this bias to encourage donations. They share simple, personal stories to explain the charity's causes. The stories often focus on a particular person. For example, a charity called *Watsi* aims to raise **funds** to help people who need an **operation** or other

---

¹**charity** (n) an organization that provides help and raises money for those in need

²**revenue** (n) money that a company receives as a result of doing business

Natural disasters, weather events, and political instability interfere with children's education around the world. Refika's school was destroyed by an earthquake.

Truth effect

DONATE NOW!

DONATE MONTHLY

$25 per month

$40 per month
(most popular option)

$50 per month

Anchor effect

Donate for children in need.

YOU CAN HELP KEEP CHILDREN LIKE REFIKA IN SCHOOL EVEN DURING TIMES OF CRISIS.

Join the more than 150,000 people who have donated this year to help keep children in school in times of crisis.

Framing effect

Bandwagon effect

medical care. On its website, you might read the story of a young student from Kenya who broke a leg in a motorcycle accident. He needs to get better soon so he can finish college and earn enough to help his family. Cognitive biases push many of us to react positively to stories like this. And other cognitive biases make us feel **sympathy** when we learn that a specific person needs help.

4   Charities may also use a cognitive bias called the "framing effect." This effect influences the decisions we make and how we make them. In simple terms, we react more positively to information with an upbeat[3] message. Look at these two statements: "Please donate your used eyeglasses to help more students see clearly" and "Your used eyeglasses might help somebody in need." The two statements mean basically the same. And if you think about the words carefully, neither statement is more likely to **persuade** people to donate. However, cognitive biases work when you read without thinking deeply. The first statement, which is from the website *Sight Learning*, a charity started by a teenager, is more likely to encourage people to give because it's more positive: That's the framing effect in action.

5   Once we decide to donate money, charities hope we will give as much as we can. They get us to give more through two cognitive biases: the "bandwagon effect" and "anchoring." The bandwagon effect means we are more likely to do something if we think a lot of other people are doing it. Everyone wants to be on the bandwagon. And *anchoring* is the way we often use the first thing we learn about something to help us make a decision. Charities take advantage of these cognitive biases with messages such as "Many people donate an average of $47." The phrase "many people" causes the bandwagon effect. And "$47" is anchor information that makes donors think around $50 is a **reasonable** donation. If the anchor figure were "$17" instead, **donors** might think a smaller amount, say $20, would be fine.

6   When charities receive donations, they and the people they support benefit. In addition, studies show that people who give to others are happier and more content, so donating benefits the giver, too. With these advantages, it's clear that the effect of some of our cognitive biases helps charities and us as well.

---

[3]**upbeat** (adj) positive

B MAIN IDEAS Number the statements from 1 to 4 in the order they are mentioned in the article. Two statements are extra.

a. _____ Cognitive biases help our brains deal with difficult problems quickly.

b. _____ College students are less affected by cognitive biases than other people.

c. _____ Donors who think others have given a lot are more likely to do the same.

d. _____ If charities tell the story of one person, donors are more likely to give.

e. _____ Messages that charities express in a positive way have a better impact.

f. _____ People who are happy give more to charities than people who are sad.

C DETAILS Match each description to the name of a cognitive bias from the article.

a. Anchoring   b. Bandwagon effect   c. Framing effect   d. Truth effect

1. _____: causes people to be more willing to do something that other people are doing

2. _____: describes the effect that a number can have on what people decide to do

3. _____: explains why people have a good reaction to something positive they have read

4. _____: makes people more likely to believe something short and easy to understand

D DETAILS Use information from the article to write a description of each number or name.

1. $410 billion: _____

2. Watsi: _____

3. Sight Learning: _____

4. $50: _____

E APPLY Complete each cause-and-effect sentence with *because* or *so*. Use correct punctuation. Underline each cause.

1. Charities are always trying to get more donors _____ some people rarely or never donate.

2. A student from Kenya hasn't been able to finish college or start work _____ he had an accident.

3. Short stories about one person can make donors feel sympathy _____ charities sometimes use this kind of story on their websites.

4. _____ the framing effect means people usually react positively to positive messages, some charities try to take advantage of this cognitive bias.

5. Some charities mention a high average donation on their websites _____ other donors think that a high donation is reasonable.

REFLECT Consider the effects of cognitive biases.

Which of the cognitive biases from the two articles might have affected your behavior or decisions in the past? Choose one and make notes about what happened. Then share what you wrote in a small group.

anchoring   bandwagon effect   binary bias   framing effect   truth effect

WRITE

A young man stands in front of Flinders Street railway station, Melbourne, Australia.

UNIT TASK Write a compare-contrast essay about experiences.

You are going to write an essay about two situations you have been in or two experiences you have had. What was similar and different about the situations or experiences? How did you behave and feel each time? Use the ideas, vocabulary, and skills from the unit.

A MODEL Read the essay. What is the main idea?

Going to College: My Experience

Attending college is a major life change and often a great experience. I've been lucky to do it twice. Both experiences were exciting and gave me amazing memories. They also had some important differences that helped me understand myself.

The first time I went to college was when I was 18 and moved to Santiago, which is the capital of my country, Chile. I didn't know Santiago before I moved there, so it took me some time to get to know the city. During this time, I felt homesick. I was surprised about this because my family and home were only about one hour from Santiago. My experience at the university was mostly positive. I took interesting classes and had some excellent instructors. Unfortunately, it was a little hard for me to make friends at first. I think this is because I wasn't very confident, and I felt and acted shy and reserved. I was quite introverted, in other words.

The second time I went to college was when I was 20. I spent a year in Australia as an exchange student. I lived in Melbourne, which is a large, exciting city on the south coast. It took me some time to get used to living in Melbourne because, like Santiago, I didn't know the city before I moved there. However, unlike my first weeks in Santiago, I was surprised that I didn't feel homesick at all even though my home and family were very far away. Just like in Santiago, my classes and instructors were great. I also made good friends in Melbourne. In contrast with Santiago, though, this happened quickly. In fact, I made two good friends on my first day at the university. Living in a new country gave me freedom and confidence to behave like a new person, and I acted in much more outgoing ways.

In conclusion, I learned a lot from these two experiences. The most important thing I learned is that my behavior and personality are not fixed. Until I was 20, I thought I was an introvert. My time in Melbourne showed me that I can act like an extrovert in some situations. That knowledge has helped me become more confident and outgoing in my daily life.

WRITING SKILL   Organize a compare-contrast essay

In a compare-contrast essay, you compare how two things are similar and contrast how they are different. This type of essay can have either a **point-by-point** or a **block** structure. In both structures, the introductory paragraph introduces the topic with background information and a thesis statement. Both structures have similar concluding paragraphs that summarize the main ideas and give a final thought or opinion. Body paragraphs are organized differently:

Point-by-point structure	**Block structure**

Introductory paragraph	Introductory paragraph

Point-by-point structure

Body paragraphs
- In each, focus on one aspect of the topic (e.g., homesickness, classes, friends)
- In each, describe similarities and differences related to that aspect of the topic

Concluding paragraph

Block structure

First body paragraph
- Describe the first experience; support your points with details and examples

Second body paragraph
- Describe the second experience; say how it was similar to and different from the first.

Concluding paragraph

B ANALYZE THE MODEL Choose the correct term to complete the sentence.

The model essay has a **point-by-point / block** structure.

C APPLY Match information from the model to the Venn diagram.

a. attended college there at 20

b. didn't feel homesick at all

c. didn't know the city before moving there

d. felt homesick for a short time

e. learned from very good instructors

f. made good friends quickly

g. needed time to make good friends

h. took interesting college classes

i. took time to feel comfortable in the city

j. was introverted and lacked confidence

k. was outgoing and felt confident

l. went to college there while a teenager

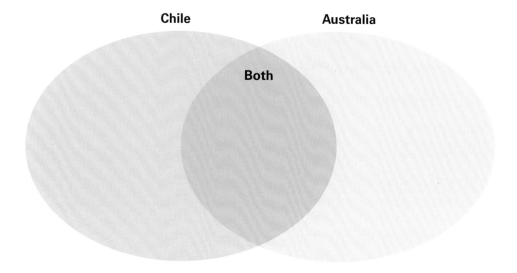

Chile   **Both**   **Australia**

D APPLY Complete the body paragraphs for an essay with the information below.

other ways	felt and behaved	in contrast	one similarity
another similarity	final difference	one difference	

My experiences living in two cities and studying at two colleges had similarities and differences.
[1]_____ was that I didn't know either city well. In Chile, I moved to Santiago.
In Australia, I lived in Melbourne. Because I didn't know either city, it took me several months to
become familiar with each place. [2]_____ was that I took really interesting
classes at both universities and learned a lot. I made great friends in both places, too. It took me
several weeks to find friends in Santiago. [3]_____, in Melbourne I made
several close friends in my first week.

　　How I [4]_____ in the two places was similar in some ways, but different
in [5]_____. One similarity was that I felt excited to start college but also a
little nervous. [6]_____ was that I was homesick during my first few months in
Santiago, while I was never homesick in Melbourne. A [7]_____ is how
I behaved. In Santiago I was reserved and introverted, but I felt like a new person in Melbourne, so
I was more outgoing. I think this is why I made friends more quickly in Australia.

GRAMMAR   Compare-and-contrast connectors

You can use various connectors to indicate ideas that are similar or different. These connectors have different grammatical functions, so it's important to study their position and punctuation as well as their meaning.

Coordinating Conjunction

I'm an introvert, **but** he's an ambivert.

Subordinating conjunctions

Although/Even though I'm an introvert, I like to spend time with some people.

Introverts like to be alone **whereas/while** some extroverts feel uncomfortable when alone.

Adverbs

I'm an introvert, and he is, **too**.

I'm an introvert. **In contrast/However**, he's an ambivert.

Introverts are good listeners. **Similarly/Likewise**, many ambiverts know when to listen.

E GRAMMAR Add the connectors from the Grammar box to the correct column. Add any other compare-and-contrast connectors you know, too.

Connectors that compare (show similarity)	Connectors that contrast (show difference)

F GRAMMAR Choose the correct connector to complete each sentence.

1. Ambiverts have traits of both introverts and extroverts. That means they enjoy time alone. **Similarly / In contrast**, they may like socializing with others.

2. Carl Jung is one of the most influential psychologists in history. The ideas of Sigmund Freud are very influential, **in contrast / too**.

3. In general, extroverts prefer talking to thinking. **On the other hand / In the same way**, introverts may think more than they talk.

4. Many people think that introverts are shy. **However / Similarly**, this is not always true.

5. Some people regularly donate to charities, **but / likewise** other people almost never give.

G GRAMMAR Complete this paragraph with compare-and-contrast connectors from the box.

likewise	however	in a similar way	but

Around the world, people have many ideas about personality. In some places, for example, people think that blood type can affect your personality. ¹_____, some people feel that the day, month, and year of your birth can affect your personality. A person born in the Year of the Tiger, for example, is likely to be brave and confident, ²_____ somebody born in the Year of the Horse often forgets things. Some people even believe that your hair color can affect who you are. ³_____, many other people feel strongly that these ideas are incorrect. They are sure personality cannot be affected by your blood type. ⁴_____, they think there is no truth to the idea that your date of birth or hair color can affect who you are.

H GRAMMAR Complete the sentences about the topic in parentheses. Use your own ideas.

1. (Two places) _____.

    Likewise, _____.

2. (Two objects) _____.

    In contrast, _____.

3. (Two people) _____,

    but _____.

WRITING TIP

To help learn and remember new expressions, it's a good idea to use them in your writing. To do this correctly, first be sure you understand the meaning of the expression. Then focus on where it typically goes in a sentence and what punctuation it needs.

I EDIT Correct the four mistakes with connectors and/or punctuation.

I find it interesting that everybody has a different personality. The other members of my family are strong introverts. They are usually quiet and are happy spending time alone, in contrast they are also comfortable talking to people they don't know. Most of the time, my behavior is introverted, likewise. But sometimes I enjoy activities that my family doesn't find comfortable, so I probably have an ambivert personality. For example, I like socializing with large groups of people. Similarly I can be very outgoing sometimes. It seems that my personality is similar to the personalities of other members of my family. Although I might be a little more of an extrovert.

PLAN & WRITE

J BRAINSTORM Complete the tasks.

1. Choose a situation you have been in or an experience that you have had at least twice.

   a. started a new job

   b. moved to a different house or apartment

   c. started a new school

   d. took part in a contest or sports event

   e. celebrated a special occasion

   f. Other: _____

2. Note down the two situations or experiences and when and where they occurred.

   One: _____

   Two: _____

3. Complete the Venn diagram. What was similar or different about the two experiences? Make notes about your actions, behavior, and feelings. Add factors—either personality or something else—that might have caused you to behave in this way.

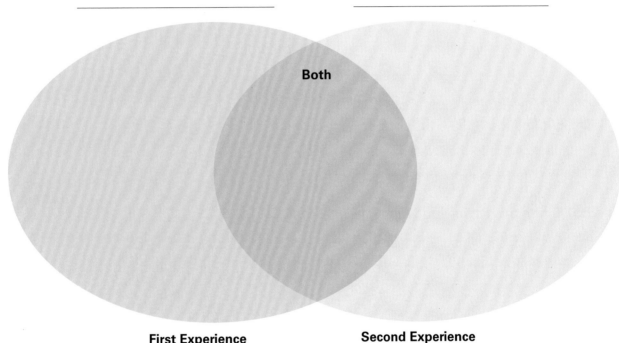

4. Choose how you want to organize your essay.

   a. a point-by-point structure that focuses on the two or three key aspects of the experience

   b. a block structure that describes the first experience in body paragraph 1 and compares and contrasts it with the second in body paragraph 2

K OUTLINE Use the structure below to write an outline in your notebook.

Introductory paragraph
General introduction to the topic and background information
Thesis statement

Body paragraph 1
(point-by-point structure) First point of comparison
OR
(block structure) First situation or experience

Body paragraph 2
(point-by-point structure) Second point of comparison
OR
(block structure) Second situation or experience

Concluding paragraph
Summary of the main ideas
Final thought or opinion about the topic

L FIRST DRAFT Use your outline to write a first draft.

M REVISE Use this list as you write your second draft.

☐ Does your essay clearly introduce what you will compare and contrast?

☐ Does it describe similarities and differences clearly?

☐ Does your essay have a clear organization?

☐ Is there any information that is not needed?

☐ Does the conclusion give a summary of the main ideas?

N EDIT Use this list as you write your final draft.

☐ Does your essay use compare-and-contrast connectors accurately and naturally?

☐ Are there any spelling or punctuation errors?

☐ Have all grammar mistakes been fixed?

O FINAL DRAFT Reread your essay and correct any errors. Then submit it to your teacher.

REFLECT

A Check (✓) the Reflect activities you can do and the academic skills you can use.

☐ compare and contrast personality types

☐ consider your behavior in different situations

☐ evaluate reasons why people help others

☐ consider the effects of cognitive biases

☐ write a compare-contrast essay about experiences

☐ recognize cause and effect

☐ organize a compare-contrast essay

☐ compare-and-contrast connectors

☐ connect information to personal experiences

B Write the vocabulary words from the unit in the correct column. Add any other words that you learned. Circle words you still need to practice.

NOUN	VERB	ADJECTIVE	ADVERB & OTHER

C Reflect on the ideas in the unit as you answer these questions.

1. What is the most important thing you learned in this unit?

2. What have you learned about how cognitive biases can affect behavior?

3. What would you like to know more about?

UNIT

8 | LEARN TO CHANGE

The Billion Oyster Project, New York City, USA
© Benjamin Von Wong | www.vonwong.com

IN THIS UNIT

▶ Assess the qualities of changemakers

▶ Describe the impact of a changemaker

▶ Consider the effects of life changes

▶ Apply advice to different situations

▶ Write a description of visuals

SKILLS

READING
Analyze visual information

WRITING
Describe data in charts

GRAMMAR
Non-defining adjective clauses

CRITICAL THINKING
Notice similarities and differences

CONNECT TO THE TOPIC

1. The Billion Oyster Project helps restore oyster habitats. How might this type of activity help change the world?

2. In general, do you find change easy or hard to deal with?

MORE THAN PEACH

A You are going to watch a video about Bellen Woodard, who wants to change attitudes about "flesh-tone" crayons. Answer the questions. Then watch the video to confirm your ideas. ▶ 8.1

Do you think that Woodard . . .

1. wants to change the cost of or the name of some crayons? _____

2. mainly wants to help students, teachers, or both? _____

B Watch the video again. Complete each sentence with one word that you hear. ▶ 8.1

1. Bellen Woodard wants to continue to change our _____.

2. She mostly donates items to _____ and senior centers.

3. She wants to be known for her _____.

4. She mentions changing _____ one crayon at a time.

5. She says it is one step closer to _____ feeling loved.

C Discuss the questions in a small group.

1. What was the most surprising thing you learned in the video? Why?

2. Is it common for young people to make this kind of change? Why or why not?

PREPARE TO READ

A VOCABULARY Read the definitions. Then complete each sentence with the correct form of the words. One word is used twice.

---

admit (v) to agree that something is true

ambition (n) a strong desire to achieve a goal or be successful

assumption (n) something you believe to be true

degree (n) a course that you study at college, or the qualification you receive after completing a course

fund (v) to provide money to start a company or organization

gifted (adj) very intelligent or having a special talent

impressive (adj) very good or special

institute (n) an organization, such as a university

passion (n) a strong interest in (or love of) doing something

struggle (v) to try hard to do or achieve something

---

1. A common _____ is that _____ children are so smart they don't need to work hard.

2. Greta Thunberg has done some _____ things, including sailing across the Atlantic.

3. Before deciding to start a company, it's important to plan how you will _____ it.

4. We sometimes find it hard to _____ when we make a mistake.

5. "Follow your _____" is good advice if you know what you love to do.

6. Some children who are _____ study at special _____.

7. People spend three years doing a college _____ in some places, four in others.

8. The goal of some people is to become rich; other people's _____ is to help others.

9. When their lives change, some people _____ to get used to their new situation.

B PERSONALIZE Discuss these questions with a partner.

1. Who is the most **impressive** person you know? Why is he/she so special?

2. What's an example of something you have to **struggle** to do?

REFLECT Assess the qualities of changemakers.

You are going to read about changemakers—people who took action to solve problems. What qualities do you think a person needs to be a changemaker? Check the four most important qualities. Then explain your choices in a small group.

A changemaker must have . . .

☐ ambition ☐ energy ☐ knowledge ☐ passion ☐ time ☐ _____
☐ creativity ☐ experience ☐ money ☐ strength ☐ wisdom ☐ _____

YOUNG
CHANGEMAKERS

A PREVIEW Scan the article to see what each of these young people have done as changemakers. Compare your answers with a partner.

Ann Makosinski   Greta Thunberg
Dafne Almazán   Yash Gupta

1   When we hear that somebody changed the world, we typically imagine he or she must be an adult. The **assumption** is that changing the world requires experience, knowledge, and wisdom and that these things only come with age. This is not always true, though. Greta Thunberg from Sweden was named *Time* magazine's Person of the Year at the age of 16 for her continuing work to protect the environment. And Thunberg is not the only one. There are many other teenagers who may be little known but who are having a big impact on the world. Here are some of their stories.

2   Dafne Almazán, from Mexico, was a **gifted** child. She learned to read and write—without help—by the age of 3, finished high school by 10, became the youngest psychologist in the world at 15, and completed an advanced **degree** from Harvard University by 18. These accomplishments are so **impressive** that *Forbes* magazine named her one of the 50 most powerful women in Mexico. According to the magazine, her strength lies in[1] her ability to inspire others, such as the students at the CEDAT **institute** for gifted children in Mexico City. At CEDAT, Almazán teaches Mandarin and psychology. Her **passion** for teaching is important because gifted children sometimes **struggle** to fit in[2]. If this happens, they may not reach their full potential[3]. She hopes to inspire these children to make Mexico a better place.

3   Yash Gupta was born in India but moved to California with his family as a child. Gupta **admits** that he was a wild child who always wanted his own way. When he was a high school freshman, though, Gupta found a positive focus for his energy. His eyeglasses broke when he was practicing taekwondo[4]. While he was waiting for his new glasses to arrive, Gupta found it difficult to focus on studying because he could not see clearly. He wondered if others might have the same problem, so he did some research and discovered that at least 12 million children needed glasses but could not get them. This inspired Gupta to start a not-for-profit organization called Sight Learning. He **funded** it with his own savings and money he earned as a tutor. Since 2010, Sight Learning has donated over 60,000 pairs of old glasses to children in many parts of the world.

[1]**lie in** (v phr) to be in; to be reflected in
[2]**fit in** (v phr) to feel accepted by a group of people
[3]**full potential** (n) the best that somebody can achieve
[4]**taekwondo** (n) a martial art originally from Korea

Greta Thunberg speaks at a climate-change event in Lausanne, Switzerland.

4   Canadian Ann Makosinski says she started inventing simple things when she was a young child. Her hobby quickly became a passion. Before she reached her teens, for example, she won a prize at a local science fair for a radio that used heat from a candle for its power source. When Makosinski's friends in the Philippines complained that they couldn't do homework because there was not enough light to study after dark, she wanted to help. She invented a flashlight that uses body heat as a source of power: Hold it and the heat from your hand makes it light up. Her design won a prize at the Google Science Fair just before her 16th birthday. Makosinski's **ambition** is to bring the flashlight to market so it can help people all over the world. She's also coming up with new inventions such as a cup that uses the heat from tea or coffee to charge a phone.

5   Dafne Almazán, Yash Gupta, and Ann Makosinski are certainly not as well known as Greta Thunberg, and it may be too early to say that they will change the world. However, they have definitely made a great start. Through their efforts, they may inspire other young changemakers to make the world a better place.

Changemakers by the Numbers

Dafne Almazán

2 Number of siblings, both of whom are also gifted

5 Languages she knows: English, French, Latin, Mandarin, Spanish

9.5 out of **10** Average grades in high school, which she finished in two years

10 Age when she began university. (Youngest in Mexico ever.)

2020 When she graduated from Harvard University

Yash Gupta

7 Days he had to wait for his new glasses

14 Age when he started his not-for-profit organization

2013 When President Obama honored him for his work

60,000 + Pairs of glasses donated to children (as of 2021)

$2 million + Value of glasses donated by his organization (as of 2021)

Ann Makosinski

1 Number of planets named after her

12 Age when she won first science competition

2017 Invented the *eDrink* coffee cup that charges phones

$5,000 Amount given for her education after appearing on "The Tonight Show"

3 million + How many times people have watched the video of her TEDxTeen talk

B MAIN IDEAS Complete the sentence about the overall main idea of the article.

It's possible for young people to have a(n) _____ on the world.

C MAIN IDEAS Choose the three statements that best summarize the main ideas.

1. _____ A negative experience inspired Yash Gupta to help children who cannot see well.
2. _____ Ann Makosinski loves inventing things that help solve problems people have.
3. _____ Dafne Almazán wants to help smart children in Mexico be successful.
4. _____ In general, young people are better at changing the world than adults.
5. _____ It's easy for Greta Thunberg to change things because she is well known.

D DETAILS Write the paragraph number where you can find each piece of information.

1. _____ A common idea about the typical age of people who change the world
2. _____ An idea that sounds perfect for people who love coffee and their phone
3. _____ The names of two educational institutions located in different countries
4. _____ The number of young people who need help in order to see clearly
5. _____ Two prizes that somebody won for turning clever ideas into designs
6. _____ Two ways that somebody helped support a project financially

---

CRITICAL THINKING   Notice similarities and differences

When you read an article that describes different people, places, or events, look for how the author compares and contrasts them. Doing so can give you a deeper understanding of the article. Sometimes the author will introduce similarities and differences with expressions such as *Similarly*, *In contrast*, or *Unlike*. Often, though, you may need to infer similarities and differences. For example, in the article you can infer that both Makosinski and Gupta got their ideas to make a change after learning about a problem. However, the article does not explicitly state this similarity.

E DETAILS Answer the questions using information from the article. Write up to three letters (a–d) for each answer.

a. Ann Makosinski   b. Dafne Almazán   c. Greta Thunberg   d. Yash Gupta

1. _____ Who achieved something impressive before becoming a teenager?

2. _____ Who did some research before deciding to take action?

3. _____ Who was described by a magazine as somebody important or special?

4. _____ Who is making or doing things to benefit the environment?

5. _____ Who is trying to improve the lives of children?

READING SKILL   Analyze visual information

Some reading texts are supported by a visual such as a map, graph, diagram, or infographic. As you read, analyze the information in the visual and compare it with information in the text. Think about how the information from both sources is related and why the visual is included.

▸ The visual includes the same data as in the reading.
  Reading: *"Sales rose by 25 percent."*
  Visual: *A bar chart showing sales up by 25 percent*

▸ The visual gives more specific data than is mentioned in the reading.
  Reading: *"three Asian countries"*
  Visual: *labeled maps of China, Thailand, and Vietnam*

▸ The visual adds data that is completely new but still relevant to the reading.
  Reading: *"College enrollments in the United States"*
  Visual: *A line graph showing college enrollments in Europe*

F APPLY Where can you find each piece of information? Write the numbers 1–9 in the correct column.

in the reading only	in the infographic only	in the reading and the infographic

1. Dafne Almazán's age when she graduated from Harvard

2. How long Yash Gupta waited for his new glasses

3. How many brothers and sisters Dafne Almazán has

4. How old Ann Makosinski was when she began inventing

5. The amount Ann Makosinski received after being on TV

6. The number of children who need help to see clearly

7. The year when Yash Gupta met the U.S. President

8. When Ann Makosinski had her idea for an *eDrink* cup

9. Which languages Dafne Almazán can speak

REFLECT   Describe the impact of a changemaker.

Think of a person you know about who has been a changemaker—someone who changed your life, your school, your city, or the world. Write notes in response to these questions. Then share your ideas with a partner.

1. What did this person change? How did he/she change it?

2. How old was this person when he/she had an impact? Was the person's age an important factor in making the change happen? Explain.

3. Did the change affect you personally? How do you feel about the change?

PREPARE TO READ

A VOCABULARY Read the sentences. Discuss the meaning of the bold words with a partner. Then write each bold word next to its definition.

- ▸ It's important to keep up with school work so that it doesn't **build up** and become overwhelming.
- ▸ It's important to eat healthy foods, but you should **vary** what you eat to avoid getting bored.
- ▸ Following a daily **routine** may seem boring, but, in some cases, it can boost creativity.
- ▸ In the past, the daily **repetition** of facts was seen as a good way for children to learn.
- ▸ A **moderate** amount of daily exercise is good for your brain and your body.
- ▸ Traveling can be a **source** of stress for many people.
- ▸ People often find it hard to **adjust** when they travel to a new time zone.
- ▸ Some busy parents have to **schedule** when to spend time with their kids.
- ▸ Some people have a **recurring** dream that they experience regularly.
- ▸ The idea that we only use one-tenth of our brain **capacity** is untrue.

1. _____ (adj) happening again and again
2. _____ (n) the place that something comes from
3. _____ (n) a regular order or sequence of events
4. _____ (n) the act of doing or saying the same thing
5. _____ (n) the amount that something can contain
6. _____ (v) to arrange for something to happen at a specific time
7. _____ (v phr) to gradually increase
8. _____ (v) to become comfortable with a new situation
9. _____ (v) to change
10. _____ (adj) average

B PERSONALIZE Discuss these questions with a partner.

1. What is something you've had difficulty **adjusting** to?
2. Do you think it's important to **build up** a personal savings account? Explain.
3. Do you have a **moderate** or a strong interest in schoolwork?
4. How can you **vary** your daily **routine**?

REFLECT   Consider the effects of life changes.

You're going to read an article about a major life change—going to college. Make a list of other life changes. Discuss the benefits and challenges of each change with a partner.

_____

_____

A STEP TO COLLEGE SUCCESS

Annenberg Hall, Harvard University, Cambridge, Massachusetts, USA

A PREDICT Look at the photo and title of the article. Make a list of ten words that you think the writer will use in the article. As you read, check if any of these words are in the reading.

1   Going to college can be a great experience. Like other positive life events, such as getting married or starting a new job, your time at college will change you in many ways. You'll make friends—and memories—that will last a lifetime. However, any major life change can also be a **source** of stress, and going to college is no different. Studies show that 75 percent of college students are concerned about studying and other academic issues. Many are also worried about other things such as staying healthy and **adjusting** to life on campus. Fortunately, creating and following a **routine** is an easy step you can take toward college success.

2   There are several reasons why routines can be effective. First, the **repetition** of doing the same things at the same times tells your brain that these activities are important, which helps them become habits. Second, because your brain is good at handling **recurring** tasks automatically, following a routine means you can spend less time and energy thinking about what to do or how to do it. As a result, you'll have more mental **capacity** for other tasks. Finally, studies suggest that routines can reduce stress levels and help people feel more positive about life in general.

3   You've come to college to study, and if you don't do schoolwork regularly, you may experience a stressful end-of-semester crunch[1]. So it's important that studying be part of your routine. This can be as simple as making and following a weekly study plan. If you procrastinate[2] or find it hard to concentrate, the *pomodoro* method may help. It involves dividing your time into blocks of 25 and 5 minutes. For example, you might do some research or other work for 25 minutes and then take a five-minute break. After that, you would repeat the 25:5 work-break cycle several more times before taking a longer break of 15 to 30 minutes.

[1]**crunch** (n) a difficult situation caused by not having enough time
[2]**procrastinate** (v) to delay something that you don't want to do

College Students' Main Concerns

📚	**75%** Studying	🏫 **33%** College Environment
65% Relationships	🔄	💵 **18%** Money
🕐	**38%** Time	❤️ **13%** Health

Figure 1

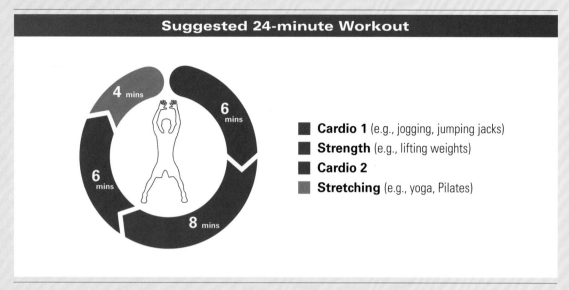

Suggested 24-minute Workout

4 mins

6 mins

6 mins

8 mins

- ■ **Cardio 1** (e.g., jogging, jumping jacks)
- ■ **Strength** (e.g., lifting weights)
- ■ **Cardio 2**
- ■ **Stretching** (e.g., yoga, Pilates)

Figure 2

4   It's important to stay physically and mentally healthy at college—around 15 percent of students worry about their health—so make sure you **schedule** time to exercise and eat right. Research shows that exercising regularly improves your physical and mental health *and* helps you study better. The latest guidelines suggest that 150 minutes of **moderate** exercise a week is enough. That's under 25 minutes per day, so a workout could fit perfectly into a *pomodoro* long break. And after a workout or a class, make healthy eating part of your routine, too. For example, if you finish class on Mondays at 12:30 p.m., plan to bring a healthy lunch to eat with friends. It may seem too much to schedule *what* you eat each day, but some people find that avoiding or choosing certain foods on certain days—*meatless Mondays*, for example—can help them eat a balanced diet[3].

5   If you're like many students, being at college is your first experience of living alone. This gives you freedom, which can be wonderful, but a disadvantage is that nobody else will do your chores, and you may be too busy to relax. Everyday tasks such as cleaning and organizing are not exciting, but if you let them **build up**, they can be a real source of stress. The solution is to include time for chores on your schedule. If you have a two-hour gap between classes on a Thursday afternoon, why not use that time to wash your clothes? Finally, college life should be fun, too, and relaxation is important for your physical and mental health. So make sure you get enough sleep and, of course, schedule time to spend with friends.

6   Creating a routine is designed to help you manage your time—a concern of almost four in ten students—but it can also take time before you feel the benefits, so keep following it for a few weeks at least. And if you find that your routine isn't working after that time, don't give up! What works for one person may not work for everybody, so **vary** your routine and keep trying to find one that works for you.

---

[3]**balanced diet** (n phr) a combination of different foods that are good for the body

B MAIN IDEAS Who do you think the article was written for? Be prepared to explain your answer.

a. Health experts who work at a college

b. Parents with children who are at college

c. Students who are about to start college

C MAIN IDEAS Write the paragraph number (2–5) next to the heading that best summarizes its main idea. One heading is extra.

a. _____ Eat Well and Keep Yourself in Shape

b. _____ It's Not What You Do, It's How You Do It

c. _____ Make Time for Chores . . . and Time for Fun

d. _____ Remember Your Reason for Coming to College

e. _____ Why It's Good to Adopt and Follow a Routine

D DETAILS Scan the article. Complete each sentence with two words from the article.

1. Any big _____ can cause stress.

2. Routines can help students achieve _____.

3. The brain can deal with _____ well.

4. Take a _____ after a few 25:5 cycles.

5. Do about 25 minutes of _____ each day.

6. Eating _____ on specific days can help.

7. If _____ build up, it can be stressful.

8. Follow a routine for a _____ to benefit.

E Look again at the two visuals in the reading. Choose the correct number to complete each statement.

1. Figure **1 / 2** includes some data that is the same as information in the reading.

2. Figure **1 / 2** gives more specific details about information from the reading.

3. Figure **1 / 2** adds new data that is relevant to the theme of the reading.

REFLECT Apply advice to different situations.

Going to college is a major life change. What ideas from the reading might help a person who is experiencing a different major life change? What other advice might be helpful for him/her? Make some notes. Then share your ideas in a small group.

WRITE

Write a description of visuals.

You are going to write a description of two charts that show information related to education. Use the ideas, vocabulary, and skills from the unit.

Most Popular University Subjects in the U.K. (% of responses)

A MODEL Look at the two charts and then read the model. Does the model mainly describe the 2010 chart, the 2019 chart, or both charts?

Trends in College Subjects: 2010 to 2019

These two bar charts show the eight most popular university subjects among students in the U.K. in 2010 and 2019. The general trend was for these eight subjects to become more popular. However, some of them changed position, and one declined in popularity.

The top eight courses did not change from 2010 to 2019, but some subjects changed positions. Medicine, which includes nursing and dentistry, and business, which includes management and administration, were the top two in both years. In 2010, design was third and biology was fourth. In 2019, however, these two subjects changed positions. Social studies was the fifth choice in both years, but the bottom three subjects changed. Technology moved from last position in 2010 to sixth position in 2019. In contrast, engineering and law each dropped one position.

Most subjects increased in overall popularity between 2010 and 2019. Biology had the biggest increase, going up by 3.6 percent to 11.8 percent. Medicine, which increased by just over 2 percent, had the second-largest rise. Social studies and technology both increased by 1.7 percent, and business and law both rose by 1.3 percent. Engineering also became more popular overall but had the smallest rise of just 0.9 percent. Design was the only subject to become less popular between 2010 and 2019. It showed a small decrease in popularity of about half a percent.

WRITING SKILL   Describe data in charts

You may have to describe two graphs, charts, or other visuals for a class or on a standardized test. A good description will typically include:

An **introductory paragraph** that summarizes what the graphs, charts, or other visuals show. You should include one or two sentences that state the main trends or points.

Two **body paragraphs** that describe key information such as changes over time, similarities and differences, and highest and lowest values. You can organize your body paragraphs in two ways.

Method 1
First body paragraph
Describe the first visual.
Second body paragraph
Compare and contrast information from the second visual with the first visual.

Method 2
First body paragraph
Compare and contrast one piece of information that is in both visuals.
Second body paragraph
Compare and contrast a different piece of information that is in both visuals.

Unlike in other kinds of writing, you often don't need a conclusion. You will generally not need to express personal opinions about the information, either, or give reasons for any changes or trends *unless* the visual includes information about those reasons.

B ANALYZE THE MODEL How is the model organized? Choose the correct method.

Method 1 / Method 2

There are several ways you can express percentages. Try to vary which ones you use:

▶ 10 percent/one in ten/one-tenth

▶ 19.7 percent/almost 20 percent/nearly one in five

▶ 25 percent/one in four/one-quarter

▶ 66 percent/two out of three/two-thirds

Use certain prepositions before percentages to express important information:

▶ use *by* (with passives) to say how many people

▶ use *by* for the amount of an increase/decrease

▶ use *from* to indicate the original number

▶ use *to* for the new number

*was chosen **by** 9 percent of participants*

*went down **by** one-fifth*

*increased **from** 3 percent*

*declined **to** 12.3 percent*

C APPLY Below are two paragraphs that also describe the charts presented in the model. Complete them with the numbers in the box. Use information from the bar charts in the model to help you.

14.5 percent	one in ten	from 8.2 percent
bottom three	to 10 percent	one in twenty
by 12.4 percent	by 1.7 percent	top two

In 2010, the ¹_____ subjects were medicine and business. Medicine was chosen ²_____ of students and business by 11.3 percent. The next two subjects were art and design, which about ³_____ picked, and biology, which 8.2 percent chose. Social studies and engineering were fifth and sixth. Almost 8 percent chose the former, and about 5 percent chose the latter. The two least popular subjects were law and technology. Both were chosen by fewer than ⁴_____ students.

In 2019, medicine and business not only remained the top subjects but also became more popular. Medicine was the choice of ⁵_____ of students, with 12.6 percent selecting business. Design and biology remained third and fourth, but their positions changed. Almost 12 percent chose biology, which is up ⁶_____. In contrast, design, which was the only subject to decline in popularity, dropped ⁷_____. Social studies remained fifth and rose ⁸_____ to 9.6 percent. Among the ⁹_____ subjects, technology moved to sixth, while engineering and law each dropped one place.

D ANALYZE THE MODEL Are the body paragraphs in activity C organized in the same way as the model?

GRAMMAR   Non-defining adjective clauses

A non-defining adjective clause gives extra information about a noun. It comes right after the noun it describes and is separated from the rest of the sentence by commas. Non-defining adjective clauses begin with a relative pronoun: *who* for people and *which* for things. Unlike in defining adjective clauses, *that* cannot be used as the relative pronoun.

> The chart**, which includes data for two years,** *shows changes in online learning.*

Because the information in non-defining adjective clauses is extra, it can be removed and the sentence will still be grammatically correct and its meaning will be clear.

> The graph**, which shows how education has changed,** *has interesting information.*
> The graph has interesting information.

Remember not to add a subject noun or pronoun after *who* or *which* when the relative pronoun is the subject of the clause:

> The photo shows Greta Thunberg**, who ~~she~~ comes from Sweden.**

E   GRAMMAR Underline three non-defining adjective clauses in the model.

F   GRAMMAR Complete each sentence with a non-defining adjective clause. Use the words in parentheses and *who* or *which*.

1. Greta Thunberg, _____, is a climate activist.

    (rowed across / in 2019 / the Atlantic)

2. Dafne Almazán, _____, was born in Mexico.

    (at / Harvard University / studied)

3. Sight Learning, _____, was started by Yash Gupta.

    (an organization / helps children / is / that)

4. Ann Makosinski's invention, _____, is a flashlight.

    (body heat / for power / uses)

5. The stories of Thunberg, Almazán, Gupta, and Makosinski, _____, are very inspiring.

    (all / are / still / young)

6. Going to college, _____, is a rewarding experience.

    (can / stressful / be / at times)

G GRAMMAR Rewrite each sentence with a non-defining adjective clause from the box. Add commas in the correct positions. One clause is extra.

which is an amazing idea	which is on the second floor	which is in England
who are living in Chile now	who has not seen it yet	who started 27 years ago

1. My friends used to live in South Korea.

   _____

2. The teacher is planning to retire next year.

   _____

3. Her invention turns banana skins into plastic.

   _____

4. Today's class will take place in room 27B.

   _____

5. The University of Oxford is very well known.

   _____

H EDIT Find and correct five mistakes with non-defining adjective clauses.

This chart, that is based on data from an academic article published in 2012, shows six main concerns that college students have. Studying, which it is the number one concern, is an issue for three-quarters of students. About two-thirds of students are also concerned about relationship issues, who probably include relationships with friends, teachers, and family members. The next two concerns are time which is a worry for almost four in ten students and the college environment, which concerns one in three students. The final two concerns are money and health which, worry 18 percent and 13 percent of college students.

PLAN & WRITE

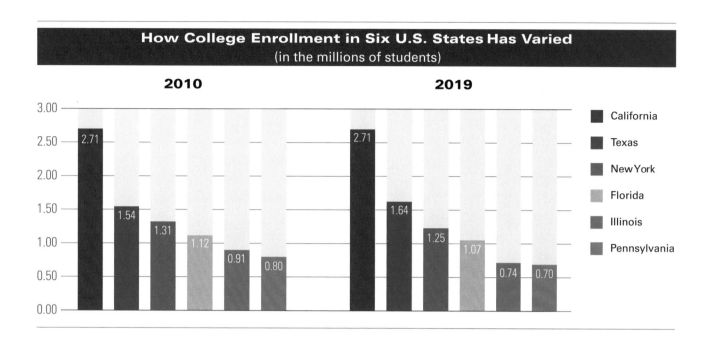

How College Enrollment in Six U.S. States Has Varied
(in the millions of students)

2010 — California 2.71, Texas 1.54, New York 1.31, Florida 1.12, Illinois 0.91, Pennsylvania 0.80

2019 — California 2.71, Texas 1.64, New York 1.25, Florida 1.07, Illinois 0.74, Pennsylvania 0.70

Legend: California, Texas, New York, Florida, Illinois, Pennsylvania

I   ANALYZE Look at the bar charts. Note trends, similarities, and differences in the information.

Trends	
Similarities	
Differences	

WRITING TIP

As you write your description, imagine that your reader cannot see the graphs or charts. This will help you write clearly so your reader can "see" the graphs or charts in his/her mind.

J OUTLINE Use one of the methods below to write an outline in your notebook.

Introductory paragraph
>   Summarize what the charts show; state the main trends or points

First body paragraph
>   Method 1: Describe the main information from the first visual.
>   Method 2: Compare and contrast one piece of information that is in
>   both visuals.

Second body paragraph
>   Method 1: Compare and contrast the main information from the second
>   visual with the first visual.
>   Method 2: Compare and contrast a different piece of information that is in
>   both visuals.

K FIRST DRAFT Use your outline to write a first draft of your description of the two visuals.

L REVISE Use this list as you write your second draft.

☐ Does the introduction describe the two charts in general terms?

☐ Are the body paragraphs organized with Method 1 or Method 2?

☐ Do the body paragraphs clearly describe any differences or similarities?

☐ Do the body paragraphs clearly describe any changes or trends?

☐ Does your description help the reader "see" the charts in his/her mind?

M EDIT Use this list as you write your final draft.

☐ Does your description use non-defining adjective clauses correctly?

☐ Are there any spelling or punctuation errors?

☐ Have all grammar mistakes been fixed?

N FINAL DRAFT Reread your description and correct any errors. Then submit it to your teacher.

REFLECT

A Check (✓) the Reflect activities you can do and the academic skills you can use.

☐ assess the qualities of changemakers   ☐ analyze visual information

☐ describe the impact of a changemaker   ☐ describe data in charts

☐ consider the effects of life changes   ☐ non-defining adjective clauses

☐ apply advice to different situations   ☐ notice similarities and differences

☐ write a description of visuals

B Write the vocabulary words from the unit in the correct column. Add any other words that you learned. Circle words you still need to practice.

NOUN	VERB	ADJECTIVE	ADVERB & OTHER

C Reflect on the ideas in the unit as you answer these questions.

1. What is the most important thing you learned in this unit?

   _____

   _____

2. Do you think following a daily routine would benefit you now?

   _____

   _____

3. What major life change do you think you will experience next? How will you deal with it?

   _____

   _____

Using a dictionary Antonyms

Antonyms are words—especially adjectives and adverbs—that have opposite or near opposite meanings. For example, the words *tall* and *short* are antonyms.

You can use a dictionary to find antonyms for common words. Antonyms are labeled *ANT* and may be listed after a definition for the word or included in a *Thesaurus* box near the word. You can also look for antonyms in a thesaurus.

THESAURUS

tall *adj.* **1** high **ANT** short

An antonym can sometimes be made by adding a prefix to an adjective or adverb. The most common prefixes are *un-* and *non-*, meaning "not," but other prefixes are possible.

likely—**un**likely   possible—**im**possible

functioning—**non**functioning   ability—**in**ability

A Match each word with the correct antonym. Use a dictionary.

1. rural _____	a. playful		6. flexibly _____	f. public
2. beneficial _____	b. closed		7. fast _____	g. unusual
3. virtual _____	c. harmful		8. private _____	h. slowly
4. open _____	d. urban		9. straight _____	i. bent
5. serious _____	e. real		10. familiar _____	j. stiffly

B Choose the correct antonym for the adjectives in bold. Check your answers in a dictionary.

1. **typical**	a. imtypical	b. atypical	c. intypical
2. **likely**	a. unlikely	b. nonlikely	c. alikely
3. **advanced**	a. iladvanced	b. unadvanced	c. inadvanced
4. **flexible**	a. inflexible	b. aflexible	c. imflexible
5. **beneficial**	a. nonbeneficial	b. abeneficial	c. inbeneficial
6. **prepared**	a. nonprepared	b. inprepared	c. unprepared
7. **perfect**	a. imperfect	b. nonperfect	c. unperfect
8. **patient**	a. nonpatient	b. apatient	c. impatient
9. **convenient**	a. inconvenient	b. unconvenient	c. nonconvenient
10. **comfortable**	a. incomfortable	b. imcomfortable	c. uncomfortable

Base words and affixes

A base word is a word that can't be broken into smaller words. For example, *decide* is a base word. You can sometimes add affixes—suffixes (dec**ision**) or prefixes (**un**decided)—to base words to form new words. Base words can also be combined to form compound nouns.

A   Which words below can't be broken into smaller parts? Check your answers in a dictionary.

1. _____ guideline

2. _____ national

3. _____ symbol

4. _____ value

5. _____ announce

B   Underline the base word in the words below.

1. interesting

2. excitement

3. suitable

4. respectable

5. profitable

6. powerful

C   Add the correct affix to each base word. You can use one of the affixes more than once. Check your answers in a dictionary.

-able	-ly	-ize	-ment	in-

1. accomplish _____

2. financial _____

3. _____ sensitive

4. official _____

5. urban _____

Greek and Latin Roots *mot* and *cycl*

Many words in English are formed from Latin and Greek word roots. Knowing the meaning of these word roots can help you understand the meaning of unfamiliar vocabulary.

The root word *mot* comes from the Latin for "moving."

The root word *cycl* comes from the Greek for "circle."

A Read the sentences and answer the questions about the words in bold. Then check your answers in a dictionary.

1. In some parts of the world, the changing of the seasons (spring, summer, fall, winter) is a **cyclical** process.

   What is a **cyclical** process? _____

2. Traveling on a boat or ship gives some people **motion** sickness.

   What is it about boats and ships that causes **motion** sickness? _____

3. Because of low wages, many workers are not **motivated** and may not work hard.

   What do **motivated** workers do? _____

4. The goalkeeper was **motionless** when the soccer player took the shot.

   What was the **motionless** goalkeeper doing? _____

5. The **cyclone** moved quickly through the town, destroying dozens of houses.

   What is a **cyclone**? _____

B Guess the meaning of the words in bold. Check your answers in a dictionary. Then write an answer for each question.

1. What is a vehicle that isn't **motorized**?

   _____

2. Who deserves a **promotion** at a workplace you know? Why?

   _____

3. Does anyone you know own or ride a **motorcycle**?

   _____

Collocations *Adjective + preposition*

Collocations are two or more words that are used together. It's useful to learn collocations in the same way as other new vocabulary.

Some prepositions, such as *for, at, about,* and *with* join with adjectives to form collocations.

> *The new season of my favorite TV show just started. I'm really **excited about** it.*

You usually, but not always, use different collocations of adjective + preposition to talk about things (actions, events, objects) or people.

> *The taxi driver went the wrong way. I was really **annoyed with** him.*
> *The taxi driver went the wrong way. I was really **annoyed about** it.*

Here are some common adjective + preposition collocations:

afraid of (something/someone)	**happy about** (something)
angry with (someone)	**interested in** (someone/something)
angry about (something)	**optimistic about** (something)
capable of (something)	**pleased with** (something/someone)
concerned about (something/someone)	**responsible for** (something/someone)
excited about (something)	**sorry about** (something)
good at (something)	**worried about** (someone/something)
good for (someone/something)	

A Choose the correct preposition to complete each sentence.

1. Many people are angry **about** / **with** / **in** climate change.

2. Parents are responsible **about** / **at** / **for** their children.

3. Some people get annoyed **of** / **about** / **for** waiting in line.

4. Eating a variety of vegetables is good **at** / **for** / **about** you.

5. Some students are worried **for** / **with** / **about** their grades.

B Complete the sentences using a preposition and your own ideas.

1. I'm concerned _____.

2. I'm happy _____.

3. I'm interested _____.

4. I'm excited _____.

5. I'm angry _____.

Using a Dictionary: Synonyms

Synonyms are words that are similar in meaning. For example, the words *beautiful* and *attractive* are synonyms.

A dictionary includes synonyms for common words. Often, these are in a *Thesaurus* box near the word. For example:

THESAURUS

trash *n.* garbage, rubbish, litter

Some words are not exact synonyms. They may have a range of meaning, usually from "most positive" to "least positive." For example, *beautiful* and *attractive* are synonyms, but *beautiful* has a more positive meaning. Likewise, *plain* and *ugly* are synonyms, but *ugly* has a more negative meaning.

MOST POSITIVE   LEAST POSITIVE

←————————————————————→

beautiful—attractive   *plain—ugly*

A Use a dictionary. Match each word (1–5) with the correct synonym (a–e).

1. principle   a. headway

2. reliable   b. promise

3. benefit (v.)   c. rule

4. guarantee (n.)   d. dependable

5. progress (n.)   e. help

6. wisdom   f. perception

B Complete the ranges using the adjectives below. Two words are extra. Check your answers in a dictionary.

amusing	naive	pointless	trustworthy
awful	nice	sensible	useless
fantastic	okay	serious	vital

MOST POSITIVE   LEAST POSITIVE

←————————————————————————————————→

1. funny—_____   _____—somber

2. _____—important   unimportant—_____

3. _____—great   bad—_____

4. wise—_____   _____—foolish

5. _____—reliable   unreliable—_____

Compound words

A closed compound word is formed when two words are joined together to make a new word. For example, *lifetime* is a compound word. Some closed compound words, such as *part-time*, are joined with a hyphen (-).

Open compound words (*high school*, *living room*) are not joined together but are still considered compound words.

A dictionary will include common compound nouns as a separate entry. A dictionary will also tell you whether the compound word is hyphenated. For example:

big-hearted *adj.* generous, warm, friendly
living room *n.* the room in a home where people usually sit, often to talk, read, or entertain

A Match the parts of the compound words. Write the new word. Check your answers in a dictionary.

1. guide _____
2. old- _____
3. out _____
4. trust _____
5. financial _____
6. trade _____
7. pressure _____
8. long- _____
9. set _____
10. self- _____

a. book _____
b. statement _____
c. fashioned _____
d. secret _____
e. term _____
f. cooker _____
g. weigh _____
h. worthy _____
i. service _____
j. back _____

B Complete the sentences with the correct form of the compound nouns from exercise A.

1. The company released a _____ that stated its profits for last year.

2. Listening to CDs is pretty _____ these days.

3. Some people use a _____ to cook beans.

4. Despite lots of _____, NASA sent astronauts to the moon in 1969.

5. Coca-Cola won't tell anyone the recipe for their popular drink. It's a _____.

Word Forms Using the suffixes *-or, -er,* and *-ion*

You can change some verbs to nouns by adding suffixes. For example, the suffix *-ion* is used for actions, processes, or results. It can be added to some verbs—especially verbs ending in a /t/ sound—to make nouns (e.g., *construct—construction*).

For verbs ending in *-ate* or *-ute,* delete the *e* before adding *-ion* (e.g., *elevate—elevation*).

You can also add the suffixes *-er* and *-or* to some verbs to make nouns. These suffixes often refer to a person that does something. For example, a *player* is someone who *plays* a game.

Not all nouns can be formed from verbs this way. Use a dictionary to check the meaning and spelling of a word if you are not sure.

A Complete the chart. Write the correct noun forms of the verbs. Three forms are not possible to make. Check your answers in a dictionary.

Verb	Noun form with *-er/-or* (to describe a person)	Noun form with *-ion*
contribute		
create		
develop		
donate		
innovate		
investigate		
move		
operate		

B Read the statements. Decide if the words in bold are usually used to describe these people. Choose **T** for *true* or **F** for *false.* Then check your answers in a dictionary.

1. Someone who acts in a movie is called an **actor**.   **T   F**

2. If you have a reaction to bad news, you are a **reactor**.   **T   F**

3. Someone who invites someone to a party is an **inviter**.   **T   F**

4. A doctor who performs an operation on someone is called an **operator**.   **T   F**

5. A person who instructs someone how to drive is an **instructor**.   **T   F**

6. Someone who moves things for a living is a **mover**.   **T   F**

Polysemy (Multiple-meaning words)

Multiple-meaning words have the same spelling but different meanings. The meanings of these words may be similar, but they aren't exactly the same. To understand which meaning is being used, follow these steps:

1. Determine which part of speech the word is.
2. Use context clues to help you understand the meaning of the word.
3. Check the meaning of the word in a dictionary.

For example:

*His glasses showed a **reflection** of the clouds in the sky.*

You can tell from the placement of the word and its form, that *reflection* is a noun. A dictionary says that *reflection* means: **1** an image repeated on a shiny surface, **2** a deep thought, and **3** a shine.

In this example, then, *reflection* must be the first definition: the glasses are showing an image of the clouds.

A Choose the best meaning for the words in bold. Check your answers in a dictionary.

1. A surgeon needs a high **degree** of skill and training.

   Degree means:

   a. amount or intensity   b. unit of measurement   c. college diploma

2. During the meeting, the employee **admitted** that he took the money but said it was an accident.

   Admit means:

   a. reveal a secret   b. allow to enter   c. accept responsibility

3. He is well **suited** for the job. He's very good at it.

   Suit means:

   a. business clothes   b. have the right skills for   c. look good

4. The photographer **adjusted** the lights so they were brighter.

   Adjust means:

   a. feel comfortable   b. change   c. repair

5. Some comedians can do accurate **impressions** of famous celebrities.

   Impression means:

   a. feeling about someone   b. outline of an object   c. a copy of someone's behavior

VOCABULARY INDEX

Unit 1	Page	CEFR
accomplish	11	C1
advanced	5	B1
beneficial*	11	B2
bilingual	11	C1
boost	11	B2
community*	5	B2
flexible*	11	B2
function	11	C1
mental	11	B2
multicultural	11	OFF
open to	11	C1
paradox*	5	C2
powerful	5	B1
privacy	5	B2
rural*	5	B2
surrounded	5	B1
trend*	5	B1
urban	5	B2
virtual*	5	B2
warn	11	B1

Unit 2	Page	CEFR
announce	33	B1
brand	33	B2
criticize	33	B2
diverse	27	B2
divide	27	B1
found*	33	B2
fusion	27	OFF
guideline*	33	C1
illustrate	27	C1
impression	33	B2
multiple	27	C1
nation	27	B2
occur	27	B2
official	27	B2
profit	33	B2
respect	33	B1
sensitive*	33	B2
symbolize	27	OFF
trade	33	B2
values	27	B2

Unit 3	Page	CEFR
amusing	55	B1
appealing	55	B2
cycle	55	B2
element	49	B2
encourage	49	B1
exchange	49	B1
explicit	55	C2
figure	55	B1
key	49	B2
opt	55	C1
overcome	49	B2
promote	55	C1
proportion	55	C1
purchase	55	B2
range	49	B1
state	55	B2
treat	49	B2
unsuitable	49	B2
vital	49	B2
worthwhile	49	B2

Unit 4	Page	CEFR
artificial*	71	B2
capable of*	71	B2
complex	77	B2
concerned	71	B2
consequence*	77	B2
content	71	B2
direct	77	C1
distinguish	71	B2
inevitable*	77	C1
knowledge	71	B1
lack	71	B2
optimistic	77	B2
prospect*	77	B2
resemble*	71	C1
resource*	77	B2
responsibility	77	B2
turn out	71	C1
valid	71	B2
vast	77	B2
wisdom*	77	B2

*Academic words

VOCABULARY INDEX

Unit 5	Page	CEFR
advance	93	B2
approach*	99	B2
ban	93	B2
conquer	99	C1
crisis	99	B2
currently	99	B2
decade	93	B2
efficient	99	B1
equivalent*	93	C1
excess*	99	C1
feature*	93	B2
generate*	93	B2
guarantee*	99	B2
innovation	93	C1
principle*	93	C1
progress*	93	B1
release*	99	B2
store	99	B2
take into account	93	B2
unreliable*	99	B2

Unit 6	Page	CEFR
competitor	115	B1
criteria*	121	C1
decline*	121	B2
ethical	121	C2
fake	115	C1
financial*	121	B1
fix	121	B1
goods*	115	B1
in the long-term	115	B2
incentive*	121	C2
investigate*	121	B2
majority*	115	B2
outweigh	121	C1
paradise	121	C1
pressure	115	B2
review	115	B1
satisfied	115	B1
service	115	B1
set	121	B2
trustworthy	115	C1

Unit 7	Page	CEFR
comfortable	137	B2
desire	137	C1
donate*	143	B2
donor	143	C2
energetic*	137	B2
funds*	143	C1
inaccurate*	137	B2
label*	137	C2
operation	143	B1
outgoing	137	C1
pattern	143	B2
persist	137	C2
persuade	143	B1
quality	137	B2
reasonable	143	B2
recharge	137	C2
reserved	137	C2
simplify	143	C1
sympathy	143	B2
take advantage of	143	B1

Unit 8	Page	CEFR
adjust*	165	B2
admit	159	B1
ambition	159	B1
assumption*	159	C1
build up*	165	OFF
degree	159	B1
fund*	159	C1
gifted	159	C1
impressive	159	B2
institute	159	B2
moderate	165	C1
recurring	165	C2
repetition	165	C2
routine	165	B1
schedule*	165	B2
source	165	B2
struggle	159	B2
vary*	165	B2

TIPS FOR READING FLUENTLY

Reading slowly, one word at a time, makes it difficult to get an overall sense of the meaning of a text. As a result, reading becomes more challenging. In general, it's a good idea to first skim a text for the gist, and then read it again more closely so that you can focus on the most relevant details. Use these strategies to improve your reading speed:

▶ Use section headings, as well as the first and last lines of paragraphs, to help you understand how the text is organized.

▶ Read groups of words rather than individual words.

▶ Keep your eyes moving forward. Read through to the end of each sentence or paragraph instead of going back to reread words or phrases.

▶ Use clues in the text—such as bold words and words in italics—to help you know which parts might be important and worth focusing on.

▶ Skip structure words (articles, prepositions, etc.) and focus on words and phrases carrying meaning—the content words.

▶ Use context clues, affixes, and parts of speech—instead of a dictionary—to guess the meaning of unfamiliar words and phrases.

TIPS FOR READING CRITICALLY

As you read, ask yourself questions about what the writer is saying. Think about why the writer is presenting the information in the text. Important critical thinking skills for academic reading include:

▶ **Analyzing**: Examining a text closely to identify key points, similarities, and differences.

▶ **Applying**: Deciding how ideas or information might be relevant in different contexts, e.g., applying possible solutions to problems.

▶ **Evaluating**: Using evidence to decide how relevant, important, or useful something is. This often involves looking at reasons for and against something.

▶ **Inferring**: "Reading between the lines"; in other words, identifying what a writer is saying indirectly rather than directly.

▶ **Synthesizing**: Gathering appropriate information and ideas from more than one source and making a judgment, summary, or conclusion based on the information and ideas.

▶ **Personalizing/Reflecting**: Relating ideas and information in a text to your own experience and situation.

TIPS FOR NOTE-TAKING

Taking notes will help you better understand the overall meaning and organization of a text. Note-taking also enables you to record the most important information for future uses—such as when you are preparing for an exam or completing a writing assignment. Use these techniques to make your note-taking more effective:

- ▶ As you read, underline or highlight important information such as dates, names, and places.
- ▶ Take notes in the margin. Note the main idea and supporting details next to each paragraph. Also, note your own ideas or questions about the paragraph.
- ▶ On a separate piece of paper, write notes about the key points of the text in your own words. Include short headings, key words, page numbers, and quotations.
- ▶ Use a graphic organizer to summarize a text, particularly if it follows a pattern such as cause-effect, compare-contrast, or chronological sequence.
- ▶ Keep your notes brief by using abbreviations and symbols like these.

approx.	approximately	**Ch.**	Chapter	**>**	is more than
→	leads to / causes	**b/c**	because	**<**	is less than
e.g./ex.	example	**p.**	page; **pp.** pages	**~**	is approximately / about
↑	increases / increased	**w/**	with	**info**	information
↓	decreases / decreased	**re:**	regarding, concerning	**yrs.**	years
i.e.	that is / in other words	**w/o**	without	**para.**	paragraph
etc.	and others / and the rest	**incl.**	including	**excl.**	excluding
& / +	and	**=**	is the same as	**∴**	therefore

TIPS FOR ACADEMIC WRITING

There are many types of academic writing (descriptive, argumentative/persuasive, cause-effect, etc.), but most types share similar characteristics. Generally, in academic writing, you should:

- ▶ write in full sentences.
- ▶ use formal English. (Avoid slang or conversational expressions such as *kind of.*)
- ▶ be clear and coherent—keep to your main point; avoid technical words that the reader may not know.
- ▶ use connecting words or phrases and conjunctions to connect your ideas.
- ▶ have a clear point (main idea) for each paragraph.
- ▶ use a neutral point of view—avoid overuse of personal pronouns (*I, we, you*) and subjective language such as *nice* or *terrible.*
- ▶ use facts, examples, and expert opinions to support your argument.
- ▶ avoid using abbreviations or language used in texting. (Use *that is* rather than *i.e.*, and *in my opinion*, not *IMO.*)
- ▶ avoid starting sentences with *or*, *and*, or *but.*

CONNECTING WORDS & PHRASES

To give an opinion	To give examples	To link ideas/to add information
In my opinion, . . . I (generally) agree that . . . I think/feel (that) . . . I believe (that) . . . It is my personal view that . . .	An example of this is . . . Specifically, . . . For instance, . . .	Furthermore, . . . Moreover, . . . In addition, . . . Additionally, . . .
To present similar ideas	**To present different/contrasting ideas**	**To give reasons**
Similarly, . . . Both . . . and . . . Like . . . , . . . Likewise, . . .	However, . . . On the other hand, . . . In contrast, . . . Conversely, . . . Despite the fact that . . . Even though . . . Unlike . . . , ...	This is because (of) . . . This is due to . . . One reason (for this) is . . . This is a consequence of . . . For this reason, . . .
To show results or effects	**To describe a sequence**	**To conclude**
Therefore, . . . As a result, . . . Because of this, . . . If . . . , then . . .	First (of all), . . . Then / Next, / After that, . . . As soon as . . . Once . . . Finally, . . .	In conclusion, . . . In summary, . . . To conclude, . . . To summarize, . . .
To summarize/paraphrase	**To analyze and critique a text**	**To explain a concept**
Overall, the text argues that . . . The main point is . . . The author feels that . . .	The significance of . . . is . . . This is a good/poor example of. . . This is important because . . . This is a strong/weak argument because . . .	This is like a . . . Think of this as . . . Essentially, this means . . . In other words, . . .
To refer to sources	**To give evidence or present facts**	**To convey attitude**
According to . . . , In the article . . . , . . . asserts/argues/claims/ states . . . We know from . . . that . . .	There is evidence/proof . . . Studies show . . . Researchers found . . . . . . tells us/shows us/proves that . . .	Certainly, . . . Clearly, . . . Of course, . . . Sadly, . . . Surely, . . . (Un)Fortunately, . . .

Reflect is designed to provide practice for standardized exams, such as IELTS and TOEFL. This book has many activities that focus on and practice skills and question types that are needed for test success.

READING • Key Skills	IELTS	TOEFL	Page(s)
Read or skim for main ideas	x	x	6, 14, 31, 37, 52, 58, 74, 81, 97, 102, 118, 124, 141, 146, 163, 169
Read or scan for specific details	x	x	9, 14, 31, 37, 53, 58, 75, 76, 81, 97, 103, 119, 125, 141, 147, 163
Preview a text	x	x	34, 50, 56, 72, 78, 100, 116, 122, 138, 160
Predict what you will read	x	x	6, 13, 28, 94, 144, 166
Take notes about what you read or see	x	x	74, 83, 87, 175
Analyze visual information	x		164, 169, 175
Understand pronoun references		x	98, 107, 108
Recognize how information is supported	x	x	10, 15, 17
Understand vocabulary from context		x	31, 32, 37
Synthesize information	x		38, 125
Recognize coherence and cohesion		x	14, 119
Recognize a writer's purpose		x	9, 14
Recognize cause and effect	x	x	142
Make inferences	x	x	53

READING • Common Question Types	IELTS	TOEFL	Page(s)
Complete sentences, a paragraph, or a summary	x		31, 58, 74, 81, 102, 103, 107, 118, 119, 128, 150, 169, 172
Match information to categories		x	84, 103, 105, 125, 147, 150, 163, 164
Match information to a paragraph	x		14, 53, 58, 62, 119, 125, 163
Short answer	x		37, 65, 75, 97, 119, 147, 163
Multiple choice	x	x	9, 10, 38, 76, 119, 124, 169
Put information in order		x	40, 52, 53, 120, 146
Multiple response	x	x	7, 14, 31, 58, 163
Match main ideas to paragraphs or texts	x		37, 81, 141, 169
Complete a table, a chart, a diagram, or some notes	x		9, 106, 141
Judge if details are true, false, or not given	x		97, 141
Match beginnings and endings of sentences	x		97

WRITING • Key Skills	IELTS	TOEFL	Page(s)
Review and edit to fix errors	x	x	21, 43, 64, 87, 108, 130, 152, 174
Plan or outline what you will write	x	x	22, 44, 66, 87, 110, 132, 154
Brainstorm ideas	x	x	21, 43, 103, 109, 131, 153
Describe a graph, chart, or diagram	x		66, 164, 171, 175, 176
Write an essay	x	x	22, 44, 110, 154
Organize an essay	x	x	18, 106, 149
Write about a process	x		62, 65, 66
Summarize or paraphrase information	x	x	84, 87, 88
Write about problems and solutions or pros and cons	x	x	103, 110
Answer questions to give supporting details	x	x	40, 44
Make predictions	x	x	77, 81
Use personal details and examples	x	x	16

WRITING • Common Topics	IELTS	TOEFL	Page(s)
Behavior and personality or personal qualities	x	x	137, 142, 147, 159
Robots and other kinds of technology	x	x	76, 81, 88, 93
Real and online communities	x	x	10, 15, 21, 22
Change and people who have changed things	x	x	164, 165, 169
Shopping	x		120, 121, 132
Cities, countries, and cultures	x	x	11, 27, 44
The environment	x	x	103, 110
Experiences	x	x	153, 169
Inventions and innovations	x	x	93, 103
Aspects of culture	x	x	32, 44
Design	x		55, 59
Helping others	x		143
Play	x	x	54

CREDITS

Illustrations: All illustrations are owned by © Cengage.

Cover © Gallus Tannheimer; **2–3** (spread) Haykal/Moment Unreleased/Getty Images; **4** © Tasneem Alsultan; **6–7** (spread) Bettmann/Getty Images; **8** (tl) H. Armstrong Roberts/ClassicStock/Alamy Stock Photo, (cl1) Patrick Box/Gamma-Rapho/Getty Images, (cl2) sjscreens/Alamy Stock Photo, (bl) SOPA Images/LightRocket/Getty Images; **12–13** (spread) NurPhoto/Getty Images; **15** Eye Ubiquitous/Universal Images Group/Getty Images; **16** Tassii/E+/Getty Images; **20** Mayur Kakade/Moment/Getty Images; **24–25** (spread) Peter Horree/Alamy Stock Photo; **26** Roberto Machado Noa/LightRocket/Getty Images; **28–29** (spread) RB/Bauer-Griffin/GC Images/Getty Images; **32** Takatoshi Kurikawa/Alamy Stock Photo; **34–35** (spread) Sergio Azenha/Alamy Stock Photo; **36** Kyodo News/Getty Images; **39** Maria Avvakumova/ iStock Editorial/Getty Images; **41** NurPhoto/Getty Images; **46–47** (spread) © French + Tye; **48** shaunl/ iStock/Getty Images; **50–51** (spread) Tristan Fewings/Getty Images Entertainment/Getty Images; **54** Anadolu Agency/Getty Images; **55** (bl) Olekcii Mach/Alamy Stock Photo, (bc) Ekaterina Minaeva/Alamy Stock Photo, (br) 3DStock/E+/Getty Images; **56–57** (spread) Christopeh Soeder/DPA/Getty Images; **59** (bl) gchutka/E+/Getty Images, (br1) Aleksandr Davydov/Alamy Stock Photo, (br2) Westend61/Getty Images; **61** Alex Nedorez/Alamy Stock Photo; **63** Boston Globe/Getty Images; **64** wavebreakmedia/ Shutterstock.com; **68–69** (spread) Peter Rigaud/laif/Redux; **70** Harvard Microbiotics Lab/National Geographic Image Collection; **72–73** (spread) CSA Images/Vetta/Getty Images; **75** Ben Stansall/AFP/ Getty Images; **76** picture alliance/Getty Images; **78–79** (spread) The Asahi Shimbun/Getty Images; **80** Phonlamai Photo/Shutterstock.com; **82** Manjunath Kiran/AFP/Getty Images; **86** Patricia De Melo Moreira/AFP/Getty Images; **88** John Springer Collection/Corbis Historical/Getty Images; **90–91** (spread) spooh/E+/Getty Images; **94–95** (spread) Vivek Prakash/Reuters/Alamy Stock Photo; **92** inga spence/ Alamy Stock Photo; **96** Buyenlarge/Archive Photos/Getty Images; **100–101** (spread) AP Images/Peter Dejong; **104** James D. Morgan/Getty Images News/Getty Images; **106** Imaginechina Limited/Alamy Stock Photo; **112–113** (spread) © Life as Lived – Matt Moyer; **114** David McNew/Getty Images News/ Getty Images; **116–117** (spread) Ashley Cooper/Science Source; **120** Westend61/Getty Images; **122–123** (spread) New York City/Alamy Stock Photo; **126** Bloomberg/Getty Images; **127** Photonons(t)/ Superstock; **129** JeffG/Alamy Stock Photo; **130** Sergei Petrov/TASS/Getty Images; **132** Yanukit Raiva/ EyeEm/Getty Images; **134–135** (spread) © Dmitry Vasyanovich/Caters News Agency; **136** Henadzi Pechan/Alamy Stock Photo; **138–139** (spread) Joel Sartore/National Geographic Image Collection; **140** Thomas Barwick/DigitalVision/Getty Images; **144–145** (spread) Reuters/Alamy Stock Photo; **145** inset © Photo/Susan Hale Thomas; **148** CraigRJD/iStock/Getty Images; **158** ullstein bild/Getty Images; **156–157** (spread) © Benjamin Von Wong | www.vonwong.com; **160–161** (spread) Ronald Patrick/ Getty Images News/Getty Images; **162** (cl) © Talent Service (c) (CEDAT), (c) Frederick M. Brown/Getty Images Entertainment/Getty Images, (cr) Matt Crossick/Alamy Stock Photo; **166–167** (spread) Rick Friedman/Corbis News/Getty Images; **167** (b1) appleuzr/DigitalVision Vectors/Getty Images; (b2) Vladislav Popov/iStock/Getty Images; **174** Liushengfilm/Shutterstock.com.